HOW TO TRANSFER TO THE

COLLEGE

OF YOUR CHOICE

Other Books by Eric Freedman

Pioneering Michigan

On the Water Michigan

Michigan Free

Great Lakes, Great National Forests: A Recreational Guide

What to Study: 101 Fields in a Flash (with Edward Hoffman)

HOW TO TRANSFER TO THE

COLLEGE

OF YOUR CHOICE

ERIC FREEDMAN

TEN SPEED PRESS
Berkeley / Toronto

Ten Speed Press
P.O. Box 7123
Berkeley, California 94707
www.tenspeed.com

Distributed in Australia by Simon & Schuster Australia, in Canada by Ten Speed Press Canada, in New Zealand by Southern Publishers Group, in South Africa by Real Books, in Southeast Asia by Berkeley Books, and in the United Kingdom and Europe by Airlift Book Company.

Cover design: Catherine Jacobes
Book design: Paul Kepple and Timothy Crawford @ Headcase Design
Copyediting: Jean Blomquist

Library of Congress Cataloging-in-Publication Data
Freedman, Eric.
  How to transfer to the college of your choice / Eric Freedman.
     p. cm.
Includes index.
  ISBN 1-58008-316-1
  1. Students, Transfer of—United States—Handbooks, manuals, etc. 2.
College choice—United States—Handbooks, manuals, etc. 3. College
student orientation—United States—Handbooks, manuals, etc. I. Title.
  LB2360.3 .F74 2002
  378.1'6914—dc21
                            2001002798

Printed in Canada
First printing, 2001

1 2 3 4 5 6 7 8 9 10—06 05 04 03 02

DEDICATION

To the generations:

Morris and Charlotte Freedman, and Erton, Zelda, and Clara Sipher

Mary Ann Sipher

Ian Freedman, Cara Freedman, and Jennifer Gilmore

Kiersten Gilmore

CONTENTS

ACKNOWLEDGMENTS

I deeply appreciate the assistance of admissions, financial aid, student services, and academic staff and of students at my own campus, Michigan State University, and at two-year and four-year institutions across the United States and Canada. Michigan State student Jenny Kish provided valuable research assistance as well.

INTRODUCTION

The need for a how-to-transfer guide emerged from my observations teaching at Michigan State University. Many transfer students enroll in our journalism classes, arriving here from a variety of backgrounds—from private colleges and from public colleges, from community or junior colleges and from other four-year schools, from Michigan, from out of state and from foreign countries. In addition, many other potential transfer students come to campus to visit or call or e-mail with questions about our programs.

It was obvious that many college students outgrow their first choice of schools, or develop new interests that can't be met there, or feel personally, culturally, or intellectually restless. Their horizons expand. Their motivations metamorphose. Their goals evolve.

Collectively, transfers account for some of the most motivated and hardworking undergrads on U.S. and Canadian campuses. They are men and women who are willing—even eager—to dramatically change their current situation for what is often a complex blend of academic, career, or cultural reasons. They enrich the tapestry of each college they attend and share a different range of life experiences with the faculty and their fellow students. They become catalysts who frequently inspire other students to periodically reevaluate their plans and self-identities.

By definition, students who want to transfer *want* to change, yet they need guidance on how to make informed decisions about doing so. Don Asher, the author of *Cool Colleges* (Ten Speed Press, latest edition), observes, "Finding the right college should be a process of discovery." Yet valuable discoveries seldom result from random chance or so-called "good" luck. They don't fall like manna from heaven. To the contrary, a significant discovery—such as a college that fits you like a custom-tailored coat—takes planning and work.

Until now, there was no comprehensive, easy-to-use, and independent guide for prospective transfers who want to plan well and work smart. There was no road map to follow as transfers sought to assess target schools for their suitability, compatibility, and offerings—a process that isn't the same for aspiring transfers as it was for them as high school seniors. For students at two-year institutions, there were no overviews on how to maximize all available transfer-related services to best prepare them to apply for and succeed at a four-year school. There was no step-by-step guide through the complexities of the application process—which varies from college to college—to increase their odds of acceptance. There was no roundup of financial aid options for transfer students or of techniques that ensure their credits will transfer as fully as possible. And there was no book with solid, well-tested advice on how to make the most of orientation at their new campus and to smooth their transition there.

No book can answer *every* question that *every* would-be transfer student may have, but we've done our best.

In doing so, we've mined the resources, experiences, and knowledge of transfer students, staff, and faculty at two- and four-year colleges in the United States and Canada, ranging from small, private liberal arts schools to the largest public universities. No two colleges handle transfer applicants and arriving transfer students exactly the same way. Procedures, prerequisites, and requirements change as well, and a highly selective college that welcomed transfer applicants last year may decide to take few or none next year. On the other hand, a school that was tough for transfer applicants to crack last year may embrace many more next year.

Some of the colleges mentioned in the book are household names. Others will be unfamiliar to you. Some are intensely competitive, and others aren't. They were selected not to recommend them as particular schools you might consider attending, but to illustrate the diverse nature of higher education and the transfer process in the two countries, including differences in philosophy, academic approaches, options, lifestyles, and procedures.

You are beginning an exciting process of discovery. Approach the transfer process with a wide-open mind. Drop any preconceptions and stereotypes. Even if you feel "sure" about where you want to go, check out a few alternatives. Read as much as you can find in catalogs and guidebooks and on the Web about that target college—its strengths *and* weaknesses. Talk to people familiar with the campus. Do the same for at least several other schools. Visit each of them with these questions firmly in mind: Why do I think I want to transfer *here*? Do I think I will be happy and successful *here* for the next few years, and why? What *doesn't* this school offer that I'd like, and can I find those missing elements elsewhere?

Don't be afraid to return to the drawing board, to reopen your search, to refine your vision, to redetermine what you want to study, where you want to study it, and why. Don't be afraid to ask questions. The transfer process is, after all, about discovery.

①

WHY TRANSFER?

ALEXIS CHAPMAN STARTED HER COLLEGE CAREER

at a college in Oregon but quickly discovered it wasn't the right fit, academi-cally or personally. She disagreed with its curriculum requirements. She wanted to live off campus and to be able to work during school. And she disliked the campus culture.

Chapman found a better fit across the country at Green Mountain College in Vermont, where she decided to major in philosophy with a possible sculpture minor. The change reflected her "heightened commitment to pursuing environ-mental ethics," she says. "Like a lot of Vermonters, I have long been interested in and concerned with the environment. My college is environmentally centered, curriculum-wise."

There are countless combinations of reasons and motives to transfer, and each student must assess that mix in the light of individual, financial, and career imper-atives. Some are tangible and relatively easy to identify, such as comparative expenses for tuition, fees, and living, or the availability of a specific major or field of study.

Others are tougher to pinpoint, such as the degree of comfort at a college known for its liberal, conservative, or libertarian lifestyle. Some students want more structure imposed on them, others want less. Some students yearn for a religious atmosphere, feeling it would be inspirational, well structured, and liber-ating, yet others chafe in such a climate. Some students are homesick because they're far away from their families and friends, while others feel claustrophobic living too close to their parents. Some seek more camaraderie, but others prefer more privacy.

There also are factors largely outside your personal control, such as the abolition of academic or extracurricular programs. A student partway through a two-year col-lege in Michigan decided to transfer to a four-year college before finishing her asso-ciate's degree in part because it was adding to its graduation requirements.

No matter how successful you feel where you are now, you may feel impelled to change. The top blocker on the Marshall University (West Virginia) volleyball

> "If you feel like you want to transfer, don't suppress the feeling—embrace it," advises Timothy MacGregor, who transferred to Wesleyan University (Connecticut) after one unhappy year at a college in Massachusetts. "Choosing a college is a gut instinct—transferring is as well. The good news is that it's hard to make the wrong decision twice."

team, who made the Mid-American Conference All-Freshman team, decided to leave largely because she was homesick. Her coach explained: "It's just a simple case of her missing home. She didn't realize what a big impact coming here would have on her and her family."

MAKING THE DECISION TO TRANSFER

For many students, the very idea of transferring is daunting. Change seems threatening, and inertia is a strong force, tough to overcome. It often feels easiest to let things continue as they are, even if we're unhappy or at least not fully satisfied—until we *have* to make a change. Yet deep inside, we acknowledge the need to move on, to improve, to explore, to grow.

To make a smart and suitable transfer decision takes hard work—if you want to do it right. It demands effort to identify and examine potential target colleges, to complete applications, to order transcripts, to schedule campus tours and interviews, to write essays, and to solicit recommendations. It takes effort to plan for your own future, to continually reassess and update that plan, and to assert control over the direction of your education and career. It takes effort to pack up and move, physically and psychologically, to meet new people, to become involved in different activities, and to feel comfortable in new surroundings. All that is daunting too, but shouldn't deter you from switching schools.

If you start your higher education at a four-year school, odds are that you intend to finish there. If you start at a two-year college, your initial plans may be uncertain: You may intend to transfer before or after finishing an associate's degree or certificate, or your original goal could be to stop with that degree and not transfer. In either case, many types of situations and circumstances can arise that propel you to transfer.

Here's how a sampling of successful transfer students responded when asked to list their three principal reasons from a choice of twelve frequent motives for transferring: one who went from Finger Lakes Community College (New York) to Hilbert College (New York) listed completion of his associate's degree, preference for a smaller college, and family reasons. Another, who transferred from Neosho County Community College (Kansas) to Ottawa University (Kansas), put the availability of financial aid first, followed by the chance to live on campus and the draw of a larger school. And one who moved from Providence College (Rhode Island) to Wesleyan University (Connecticut) was motivated most by the desire for a smaller school, trailed by the greater prestige of his new college and access to more financial aid.

Not surprisingly, money is a frequent motivator. Tuition and fees at a community college may be half those of a nearby four-year state school, for instance. A high-caliber public institution may charge state residents under $7,500 a year for tuition and fees, while tuition and fees at some comparable—or lower-rated—private colleges are now in the $30,000-plus range and rising. Even the costs of dormitories and meal plans can vary dramatically from campus to campus.

When a star basketball forward at Independence Community College (Kansas) transferred, her selection of the University of Maryland at College Park was based primarily on its location, fifteen miles from where she grew up: "It was really important for me to come back home. For one, my family is the number one thing in my life and my goal throughout my whole life has been to play basketball in front of my family. I didn't have that opportunity right out of high school."

An athlete at Southern Illinois University, who had transferred from a two-year college in his home state of Texas, expressed similar thoughts for returning to Texas so he can help care for his orphaned brothers and sisters while attending school: "I'm going back home to be with my family. Family comes before basketball or anything."

And a basketball player who spent her first two years at Butler University (Indiana) switched to the University of Indiana at Bloomington because "I wanted to play at a bigger school and at a higher level, but still stay close to home."

Not all reasons fit neatly into categories. For example, a student who left a suburban Detroit community college to attend Michigan State University before completing her associate's degree said the principal reasons were that she "wanted a guarantee in life, wanted to make something of myself, and wanted the experience." In addition to ranking items from the suggested list of reasons, a transfer student to Texas Woman's University cited "opportunities for growth and an environment where professors work to help you understand materials and transition to graduate school."

In his book *Cool Colleges*, Don Asher recalls his own experience at a major university: "I did not adjust well. I was shocked that my fellow students were more interested in dating, sports, and avoiding the real world for four years than they were in learning. Students openly discussed cheating, and professors routinely dismissed class well before the scheduled end." Disappointed, he dropped out after one semester and eventually transferred to a "place where I would fit in, where I was the norm, where I was welcome, and where I felt at home."

While one or two factors may weigh most heavily in your mind, you must balance many considerations in determining whether or not to transfer. For instance, your current college is so expensive that you'll emerge heavily in debt with student loans, but its academic rigor, reputation, and job placement rate may help you find a higher-paying job after graduation. Or you're unhappy and lonely halfway across the country from your family, but few other colleges offer the specialized curriculum you want.

Can you come back if you feel you made a mistake? Sometimes, yes. When Miami University (Ohio) abolished its tennis program, one adversely affected player transferred to a mid-South university, only to return. "I had a great experience here," he said of Miami University after his return, "and I had made so many friends. It didn't compare to being here."

If you plan to transfer, you'll find yourself with plenty of good company. While the proportion of transfers varies from campus to campus, the number is significant at many schools. For instance, about one-third of undergraduates at Rochester Institute of Technology (New York) and more than a third of the entering students at Slippery Rock University (Pennsylvania) are transfers from a community college or another four-year institution or are returning to college after time away. The State University of New York at Plattsburgh boasts, "We are a transfer college. Half of all Plattsburgh graduates entered as transfer students. Plattsburgh annually enrolls 980 freshmen and 800 transfer students."

A recent study by the National Center for Education Statistics confirms that transfers are becoming increasingly common. Here are a few of its key findings:

- 28 percent of students who began at a four-year institution during a recent five-year period transferred, most to another four-year school
- 43 percent of students who began at a two-year school transferred
- 65 percent of students transferring from community colleges transferred without completing an associate's degree. However, those who did complete an associate's degree were more than twice as likely to finish their bachelor's after transferring.

So who is most likely to transfer? Forget the stereotypes.

Research shows that many—if not most—transfers no longer fit the stereotype of students who go to community college immediately after high school, earn an

"In retrospect, a seemingly circuitous path can prove to be the most direct. In applying to transfer, you benefit from your previous experience. You've already done a lot of research into different colleges, and have had the opportunity to explore new interests in one kind of college setting. Now you can know yourself even better than you did when you first selected that college. You also know better what information you need in order to make a decision that will bring you closer to achieving your academic and personal goals."

—Bryn Mawr College (Pennsylvania)

Warning: Don't expect a transfer to solve all your underlying problems. It won't. One admissions officer uses the term "suitcase transfers" to characterize students whose primary rationale for switching is simply to get away from an uncomfortable situation, such as a roommate conflict. That doesn't provide a compelling reason for another college, especially a competitive one, to accept you. And even if you do transfer, there's no guarantee you won't run into similar problems again.

associate's degree, and move on to a four-year institution. "Although many two-year transfers fit this profile, there is increasing evidence it is an outdated characterization," according to Professor Barbara Townsend of the University of Missouri in Columbia. She's identified a variety of other common patterns, including students who transfer to a four-year college after attending two—or more—two-year schools, students who simultaneously enroll at a four-year and a two-year institution, and so-called "reverse transfer" students who begin at a four-year college, switch to a two-year college, and then transfer back to a four-year one.

"For many students the two-year college is one of several colleges attended in a circuitous route to the baccalaureate, a route that includes frequent transferring between colleges in both the two-year and four-year sectors," Townsend writes in *College & University Journal*. "Students also transfer back and forth because there are so many institutional options available. The extensive growth of the public sector of higher education since the 1950s means that most locales typically have several colleges and universities."

REASONS FOR TRANSFERRING

The National Center for Education Statistics study found that transfers from four-year institutions frequently relate to dissatisfaction with intellectual growth, teacher ability, institutional prestige, and social life. "Of these factors, students' dissatisfaction with their intellectual growth had a very strong correspondence to transfer: Sixty-three percent of those who were dissatisfied with their intellectual growth at the first institution transferred, compared with 25 percent of students who found their intellectual growth to be satisfactory."

And students at private four-year colleges who were dissatisfied with the institution's prestige were twice as apt to go elsewhere than those who were satisfied with its prestige.

The federal study also reported that the availability of services such as job placement, personal counseling, and job counseling, together with student satisfaction, plays a key role in decisions to transfer from four-year schools.

The University of Missouri's Townsend observes, "Educational policymakers need to be more aware that many so-called drop-outs leave a particular college but do not leave higher education. Instead, they transfer to an institution that better serves their financial, academic, or even geographic needs."

Even more importantly, students need to recognize that their decision to transfer is not a symbol of failure, inadequacy, or rejection. Instead, transfers should be viewed as opportunities—to find a better intellectual, economic, or lifestyle fit, to explore and grow, and to move their lives forward.

WHEN TO TRANSFER

When you transfer is important. Do you want to plunge right in at another college, or do you want to take off a semester, a year, or even longer to work, serve in the armed forces, volunteer, or travel? Many transfer students take off for a while to earn money to help pay for their new college. It's also not unusual to take a break to reconsider what you want to study and where, especially if you feel your top targets are way off-base or out of reach.

In the National Center for Education Statistics study, students from four-year colleges were much more likely than transfers from two-year schools to enroll at their new destination within six months. Meanwhile, almost one-quarter of transfers from two-year institutions were out of school for more than three years.

You may be among those who've interrupted your higher education for many years—so-called nontraditional students—to work, serve in the armed forces,

COMMON REASONS TO TRANSFER

Transfer students list these as their most common reasons for switching schools:

ACADEMIC

- Completed a degree or certificate at their first college
- To find a major or program not offered at their current college
- More challenging academic environment
- Less competitive academic environment
- More opportunities for independent study, overseas study, cooperative learning

ECONOMIC

- More financial aid available
- Lower tuition, fees, housing, and other costs

PERSONAL & LIFESTYLE

- Family, such as ailing parents or a spouse's job
- Feel more comfortable at a larger college
- Feel more comfortable at a smaller college
- Friends at new college
- Extracurricular opportunities such as athletics, performing arts, and clubs
- Different climate
- Ease of commuting
- Availability of on-campus housing
- More lenient campus environment
- Stricter campus environment
- Larger or smaller community

CAREER

- **More prestige for graduates**
- **Career-related internships**
- **Better job placement opportunities after graduation**
- **Improved chances of acceptance to highly rated post-undergraduate opportunities, such as veterinary, business, law, or medical school or Ph.D. programs**

---

raise children, save money, or simply develop more maturity and self-direction. (The U.S. Census Bureau found that Americans are now better educated than ever before, and that in the year 2000, a record 25.6 percent of Americans twenty-five and older had graduated from college. Sixty years earlier in 1940, that figure was only 4.6 percent.)

Transfer applicants who've been out of school for a long time may be assessed differently. Rowan University (New Jersey) says, "Admission decisions for transfer applicants who've attended college more than five years ago may be based on motivation, life experiences, career development, and college transcripts."

Columbia University (New York) has a School of General Studies for nontraditional and returning students who have interrupted their formal education for at least a year. "The admissions process takes into account traditional measures of academic success such as test scores and high school grade point averages," the college says. "We will also, however, make a determined effort to engage our applicants in a dialogue designed to gauge potential to succeed. This dialogue, while not discounting traditional admissions criteria, will encompass a profile of work experiences, past academic accomplishments, depth of commitment to a demanding program of study, and personal achievement and pursuit of excellence."

You may have no choice about when to start at your new school because some colleges or individual programs accept transfer students only for the fall. For example, at Cornell University (New York), students in engineering and landscape

Words of advice: Don't act precipitously to get out of your current uncomfortable situation. Many students are initially homesick during their first few months at college, particularly if it's too far to visit family on weekends, they don't know anybody on the campus, and it's their first extended period away from home. If that description sounds familiar and you transfer after only a semester as a freshman, you may do yourself a disservice.

architecture can begin only in the fall, and transfers to its five-year architecture program can start only in the fall unless they've already completed two years in another accredited architecture program. Colleges also modify their admissions timing to balance enrollment, as Brown University (Rhode Island) did when it decided to accept more transfer students in the spring and fewer in the fall.

That may give you an unanticipated semester interruption if you finish your associate's degree in December and have eight or nine months free before you start at the new campus.

TYPES OF TRANSFERS AND TRANSFER PROGRAMS

Not all transfers fit the patterns you're most familiar with. For example, there's movement from four-year colleges to community colleges, known as reverse transfers; movement within a university system, known as intercampus transfers; and the prospect of earning degrees from two institutions at the same time, known as the dual degree option.

REVERSE TRANSFERS

These are students who move from four-year to two-year institutions, and there are plenty of them. A University of Central Florida researcher reported in *Community College Week* that one-third of the students enrolled at a community college in that state had previously attended other colleges and universities.

Reverse transfer students who haven't finished a bachelor's degree may opt for a community college to pick up an associate's degree or certificate, take courses to transfer credits elsewhere, or get back into the groove of academics after a break. Perhaps they had difficulty studying or dealing with the intellectual rigor at their first college, or they simply weren't mature enough to take it on. Also, they may find a community college more convenient, closer to home, and less expensive.

INTERCAMPUS TRANSFERS

These transfers involve moving from one campus to another under the umbrella of the same university system. Most commonly that involves public systems, either statewide (such as the California State University system) or among multiple campuses of the same institution (like Indiana University and the University of Michigan). It can happen in the private realm as well. St. John's College, which has campuses in Maryland and New Mexico, has such a process.

Motivations for intercampus transfers are similar to those underlying other transfers: money, prestige, personal and family considerations, location, and academic offerings. However, the application procedures and admissions criteria may differ from those of "outside" transfers.

DUAL DEGREES

This innovative approach allows transfer students to simultaneously earn degrees from two colleges. For example, the Affiliated College Program offered by Rensselaer Polytechnic Institute (New York) is designed for students at more than forty participating liberal arts schools, public and private. If those students are interested in engineering, they finish their first three years at their liberal arts college, then transfer to Rensselaer's engineering school for "two years of carefully planned study." At the end, they receive two bachelor's degrees.

TRANSITIONAL PROGRAMS

Say you're a nontraditional student—you interrupted your education to work, serve in the military, do full-time volunteer work, raise children, care for an ailing relative, or recover from a serious injury or illness. You may want to consider a college that offers transitional programs that will ease you into full-time studies. As an example, a continuing education center at Sarah Lawrence College (New York)

Another reason for some students to wait: **If your academic record so far is so-so or worse, you might fare better in the transfer process by spending an additional semester or year bolstering your grades, thus making you more attractive to target colleges. Chris Tillman, the assistant admissions director at Keuka College (New York), says, "Depending on the major, it may be worth staying where they are and repeating or taking certain classes. It may help them more in the transfer process."**

lets nontraditional students take a prearranged number of courses and credits for a year or two, then transfer into the college's student population.

You might also look at schools with undergraduate programs for adults. At Xavier University (Ohio), the Center for Adult and Part-time Students admits, advises, and registers undergraduate adult students who may attend part time or full time and who can take a combination of day, evening, or weekend classes. In addition, the program makes available special financial assistance and tuition grants for those students.

Since 1972, Brown University (Rhode Island) has offered what it calls the Resumed Undergraduate Education Program aimed at older students or those who have interrupted their education for at least five years. Here's how the university explains it: "Not everyone finds four or more years of college possible, or even desirable, right after high school. Because of family commitments, or financial problems, or perhaps a more compelling need to explore other paths, many men and women interrupt their formal education. Perhaps you are one of these people. Now it's five years later—or perhaps many more. You have achieved some important goals, and can be justly proud of your accomplishments. But lately you have begun thinking about the goals you can't achieve without a college degree. You may wish to widen your horizons or change direction. Maybe you have developed a serious interest in a field of inquiry that can be pursued only in a structured academic environment. Whatever the reason for your renewed interest, you are certain that you want the very best education available."

Eligibility is limited to strongly motivated applicants who are at least twenty-five or who have been out of school for five years or longer, and intend to finish their bachelor's degree. A separate admission committee reviews their credentials, and it "makes admission decisions based primarily on an appraisal of the experience, maturity, commitment and future academic potential. This means that candidates can be judged in terms of their own ability and qualifications for Brown and not considered with the applicant pool of students of traditional entering age." Those admitted through this route have the option of carrying a reduced course load.

Another approach is that of Winthrop University (South Carolina). Winthrop runs a New Start Program for prospective students twenty-five years or older, including transfers who are continuing undergraduate work begun years earlier. Transfer applicants are evaluated based on their GPAs from all previous institutions. And although they generally must meet the same requirements as traditional transfer students, Winthrop considers such factors as time elapsed since the last enrollment and life experiences.

Urban College of Boston (Massachusetts) offers a different model. This community-based, two-year institution serves nontraditional, low-income students and offers classes only on weekends and at night. It has agreements that allow its graduates to transfer directly to the University of Massachusetts at Boston, Lesley University (Massachusetts), and Wheelock College (Massachusetts).

CONTINGENCY PLANNING

Don't wear blinders during the transfer process. You may be a highly desirable recruit with all the right credentials for the "perfect" college. There's no way the school will reject you and no way you'd decide not to go there—or so you think. Yet it's important to do contingency planning because the unexpected can happen: You *do* get rejected, or the college freezes transfer admissions for the semester you planned to start there. Its financial aid package proves insufficient.

Family or employment commitments dramatically change. You suddenly decide on a different major. The college dissolves the department you intended to major in. Another college woos you with an irresistible offer. Health problems arise. As an athlete, you seriously injure yourself and won't be able to compete, or your intercollegiate team is abolished. A news story reports on an exciting new program in your intended field—but at a different college.

That's why this book urges you to explore. Visit, talk with faculty and staff, check Web sites, and read catalogs for several schools that may want you and where you'd succeed. You may surprise yourself, and you'll be better prepared for the unexpected.

Transferring colleges is an important life decision, one that's subject to lots of academic, financial, and personal considerations, as well as outside influences. Talking with students who've transferred, you'll discover that no two of them give exactly the same explanation for why and how they did it. Moments of self-doubt and uncertainty are inevitable, but don't worry. There is no magic answer, and your only real concern should be making decisions that feel right for you.

2

SO WHY DO
THEY WANT
YOU?

JUST AS THERE'S A COMPLEX MIX OF REASONS WHY

students want to transfer, there's a complex mix of reasons why *colleges* seek transfer students. They include, among others, broadening the academic caliber and life experiences of their student bodies, improving their diversity, ensuring the flow of essential tuition and fees, and strengthening their athletic teams. Often, a careful review of transfer student recruiting material or a conversation with an admissions officer will reveal what the mix of factors at a target college is and how well your credentials and attributes may help that college meet its goals.

As Harvard University (Massachusetts) puts it, "Over the years, we have found that transfer students contribute a great deal to college life here as well as gain much from their experience." Similarly, Stanford University (California) says, "Transfer students add significantly to the maturity, diversity, and academic excellence of the student body. Hence, the university is committed to making them an integral part of the undergraduate program. In evaluating academic preparation and potential, we go beyond identifying students who are capable of succeeding at Stanford and select those who have the most distinguished academic records and will add in significant ways to the life of the university."

Teresa Mauk, the director of admissions at Texas Woman's University, says, "In some ways we prefer transfer students because they've already proven themselves in the classroom. Our feeling is the attrition rate is less because they're past that freshman year. Also, we don't have many transfers who are undecided about their majors."

And the University of the Arts (Pennsylvania) says, "Transfers enjoy a preferred position among applicants for admission since it can be assumed they have matured in their goals and have demonstrated their abilities at the college level."

There are, however, rare occasions when a college decides against accepting any transfers, at least for a while. In August 2000, Princeton University (New Jersey) announced: "Because previous freshman classes exceeded our enrollment

19

goals, and because we have a very low attrition rate, it has been necessary to suspend the admission of transfer students for the foreseeable future."

Colleges, large or small, famous or little known, are proud of what they have to offer and what their alumni, their students, and their faculty have accomplished. The University of Chicago (Illinois) tells prospective applicants, "Seventy or so transfer students come to us each year, attracted to Chicago by the opportunity to explore a great city and by the chance to enjoy a talented array of friends and professors. The university has one of the best faculties in the world, 90 percent of whom teach undergraduates," and it goes on to note that seventy-one Nobel laureates "so far" have studied, taught, or done research there.

Academic experts regard the number of transfers from community and junior colleges as one indication of how well four-year colleges serve the needs of such students. That's why the State Council of Higher Education for Virginia uses the number of transfer students as one of fourteen performance measures to evaluate the state's four-year public colleges and universities.

What if you were rejected when you applied to your dream college as a high school senior? Should you abandon hope and give up?

Not necessarily. It depends on the college, according to admissions experts. For example, many successful transfer applicants to Morehouse College (Georgia) didn't make it when they tried to get in as freshmen because of low academic performance in high school but improved their grades and overall desirability after that. Admissions counselor Myron Burney says, "We find most of our transfer students have had aspirations prior to coming to the institution and are already familiar with the institution."

Bates College (Maine) makes it easier to reapply under such circumstances. If you applied within the previous two years, the college will reactivate your original application and waive the application fee, whether or not you were accepted on the first go-round. You still must submit up-to-date credentials and are strongly encouraged to provide new writing samples and recommendations. The University of Missouri at Columbia allows transfer applicants who weren't admissible directly from high school to apply if they have at least twenty-four credits and a minimum 2.0 GPA.

Yet at Williams College (Massachusetts), there's little chance of acceptance as a transfer if you didn't make the cut as a freshman applicant, unless some other underlying criterion is met, such as an alumni connection or athletic prowess. On the other hand, you may get a second shot if you were accepted as a freshman but chose to go elsewhere before realizing that Williams is where you really want to be.

One factor to look for is the proportion of transfer students already attending a target college because that suggests the relative importance the school gives to reviewing and accepting transfers.

Transfers make up a significant ratio of the student body at some schools. At the State University of New York at Oswego, that figure is about 35 percent. The college's coordinator of transfer services, Gail Akin, says that high proportion creates a "transfer-friendly" environment that, in turn, attracts more transfers.

For colleges, another consideration that reflects your desirability is that accepted transfer applicants are more likely to enroll than new high school grads. For example, Temple University (Pennsylvania) reports that 60 percent of its accepted transfer applicants attend, contrasted with 35 percent of the high school seniors who are accepted for the freshman class. At Wesleyan University (Connecticut), the comparable figures are 57 percent of transfer students who are accepted and 38 percent of freshman applicants. At the University of Chicago (Illinois), it's 60 percent of accepted transfer applicants and only 32 percent of accepted freshmen.

There are several principal reasons for this, including the fact that transfer applicants typically are more focused on where they'd like to go and more decisive when given a choice, unlike many high school seniors who take a shotgun approach to applications. Also, transfers are apt to better research prospective schools and gauge the costs of attending before they apply, making it less likely they'll apply to schools that are unsuitable or too expensive. And they're more likely to stay and graduate, demonstrating a higher retention rate than freshmen.

Those figures and the reasons behind them mean that you and other transfer applicants gain an admissions edge that you didn't have coming directly from high

Kenyon College (Ohio) explains that it "welcomes students who apply for admission after beginning undergraduate study at another institution. The admissions staff recognizes that not all students are comfortable with their initial college choice—and that academic and career goals often change during the college years."

school. That also indicates that your application may receive more careful consideration and that you have higher odds of getting into the college of your choice than you did as a freshman-to-be.

BROADER STUDENT BODY

Transfers change the dynamics and demographics of the student body at a college, enriching it with different ideas, skills, and ways of thinking. For one thing, many transfers are older than other students at the same level—sophomore or junior, most often—who arrive straight from high school. Often they have more part-time or full-time work experience. Many know firsthand the importance of money, budgeting, and struggling to make ends meet, having supported themselves in the past. Some are parents who carry the heavy responsibility of juggling a schedule filled with family, academic, and job commitments. Some have served in the military or traveled extensively.

They have the benefit of exposure to other forms of teaching at their previous colleges, and that may affect class discussions, work on projects and papers, and other assignments—thus influencing all students in their classes. As Mt. Holyoke College (Massachusetts) recognizes, "Transfer students add to the rich mix of student experience on the campus and to the intellectual and social life of the college."

Why is that good for a school? First, campuses should be marketplaces for ideas and debate, providing forums for analytical challenges. Different ways of thinking and a variety of life experiences provide grist for the intellectual mill, encouraging all students and faculty to open their minds. Second, more mature students may serve as role models for their classmates. That's why transfer students often plunge into leadership positions in campus organizations, put together study groups, and act as mentors for other students. Third, colleges build their reputations in part on the success of their graduates. Highly motivated transfer students who take their energy and learning to the workplace after graduation help build the reputations of their adopted alma maters. Finally, transfers who already have earned an associate's degree at a community or junior college arrive on their new campuses with a sense of confidence and achievement, helping to create a can-do atmosphere for their classmates.

IMPROVED DIVERSITY

Colleges face a range of pressures that affect the recruitment and acceptance of transfers. One of those pressures is the need for a diversity of students. For example, the *Chronicle of Higher Education* reported how the University of Washington is using transfer programs as a way around a 1998 referendum that bans affirmative action in admissions. That effort comes at a time when the university is confronting negative stereotypes about the campus and a decline in minority student enrollment. "Officials are now scrambling to invite more [minority] students to the campus, to assure them they are welcome, and to persuade them to enroll. For students, the route is cheaper, and sometimes easier, than competing for admission as a freshman," the newspaper reported.

Two-year institutions often serve as the University of Washington's principal recruitment pool. The *Chronicle* quotes the university's executive director of admissions and records as saying, "The community college has always played a role in providing alternate acceptance for minority students, but it has taken on a more central role as we have more restricted access to freshman enrollment." And many four-year institutions actively recruit on community and junior college campuses.

To promote diversity, the University of California system has decided to increase community college transfers by 50 percent by 2005. As part of that policy, the system has moved to extend admissions offers to all California students in the top 12.5 percent of their high school graduating class if they first finish two years at a community college in the state. "A goal here is to increase diversity, but it's diversity of low-income students, of underrepresented students, and of rural students," the president of the system, Richard Atkinson, explained. Under the plan proposed in 2000, those students would be provisionally admitted to a University of California campus. To finalize the transfer, they would need a 2.4 GPA and an approved two-year program of study at a community or junior college.

FINANCIAL BENEFITS

There's a strong financially driven competition for students, whose tuition, fees, housing payments, and state aid are essential for keeping colleges in operation and for controlling costs. Without an adequate student revenue base, private and public colleges face the disagreeable, often painful, task of laying off faculty and staff, shrinking or eliminating programs, delaying maintenance and repairs of buildings, and reducing library and database acquisitions—all of which can harm the quality of education and services there.

Other factors also drive that financial reality, including the reluctance of many state legislatures and local governments to keep public funding increases for public institutions at or above the rate of inflation. When appropriations are made, the formula usually takes into account the size of the student body. In addition, a fluctuating or hard-pressed local, regional, or national economy makes it tougher for colleges to rely on a predictable flow of grants, donations, and research contracts.

Four-year schools' escalating tuition and fees, often coupled with the cost of living in a dormitory instead of at home, lead many potential students to start at two-year colleges. One attraction of community colleges is that they're usually cheaper than four-year institutions, even public ones, so many students opt to save money by spending their first year or two at a community college. Not surprisingly, that means four-year colleges eagerly turn to transfer students to fill the gap, and often compete to woo desirable community college graduates.

In the mid-1990s, Missouri developed its A+ program in which students who graduate from certified high schools with a minimum 2.5 grade point average and a 90-percent attendance rate qualify for two years' free tuition, books, and fees at any public community college in the state. That program draws a lot of students, including some of the brightest, and leaves four-year schools scrambling to fill seats. "The four-year institutions have realized that we're starting to lose kids," says Chip Parker, the associate director of admission and transfer coordinator at Drury College (Missouri). "We'd been recruiting transfer students, but not with the time and energy we are now. We're trying to get them interested in Drury and going on to their four-year degree."

It's true that many colleges are seeking out transfer students, but don't naïvely assume that means they'll take anybody simply to fill a seat and generate tuition. However, they may work with individual applicants or with community colleges to improve the preparedness of potential transfer students and to increase the odds of their success in a new environment. At the same time, that cooperation strengthens the college's financial base through higher enrollment and improved retention.

STUDENT-ATHLETE TRANSFERS

College athletes are an important component of the transfer population, but often for reasons other than diversity or tuition revenue. That's because a network of coaches, alumni, and boosters actively recruits many of them. Also, those who do well at their current school may attract media attention, and college athletic departments monitor the press and the Internet to locate potential recruits. It's not unusual for campus and area newspapers to report when a prized transfer candidate has accepted an offer.

Beyond that, many promising athletes intentionally choose two-year schools or smaller, less athletically prominent four-year institutions to get playing experience. They realize that, fresh from high school, they're unlikely to get much game time on the field or court at a Big Ten, PAC Ten, or other mega-conference school. Instead, they opt for the chance to build their playing skills in a less intense, less competitive environment in hopes they'll be able to transfer up after a year or two. There are financial incentives for successful transfers as well, because some schools award scholarships to student-athletes.

As for academics, some research shows that athletic participation overall does not impair educational performance. In a study of grades and graduation rates at the State University of New York at Binghamton, a National Collegiate Athletic Association (NCAA) Division III school, researchers John Robst and Jack Keil found that transfer student-athletes have grades similar to those of nonathletes. In all seven women's sports covered by the research, transfer athletes had GPAs equal to or higher than female nonathlete transfers. Among men, transfer athletes' GPAs on two teams ranked at or slightly above nonathletes and slightly below on seven others. The study, published in the journal *Applied Economics*, reported that college athletes take more credits per academic year and carry more difficult course loads than nonathletes, "contradicting popular stereotypes that athletes are uninterested students who concentrate only on sports."

High-performing athletes also have more leverage—bargaining power—in the transfer process, particularly if they are strong in scholastics as well as in sports. When Swarthmore College (Pennsylvania) decided to cancel its football program in late 2000, coaches elsewhere quickly launched recruiting efforts. The *Phoenix*, the Swarthmore student newspaper, reported that disappointed players were applying to such colleges as University of Pennsylvania, Brown University (Rhode Island), Williams College (Massachusetts), Carnegie-Mellon University (Pennsylvania), Johns Hopkins University (Maryland), and Amherst College (Massachusetts). "Players say they are taking into account academic prestige as well as football in their consideration of which colleges to apply to," the *Phoenix* reported. It also quoted one football player who was "leaning toward staying" at Swarthmore: "The academics are better here than at other schools. The academics are why I came here—for the best possible education. Football is how I got in, but academics come before football."

Institutions that belong to the NCAA and the National Association of Intercollegiate Athletics (NAIA) must adhere to strict rules concerning the recruitment of transfers. For example, the NAIA prohibits athletic recruiters from discussing the possibility of transferring—including requirements, team openings, and financial aid—until the current institution has been notified of the student's declared interest—even if the target school had tried recruiting him or her directly from high school. Violators are subject to sanctions.

Overall, it's essential to evaluate yourself and your background in and out of school in a realistic way to highlight the experiences and attributes that will make a target college *want* you. What can you bring to that campus and its student body? Once you've figured this out, use the application process—including essays, recommendations, interviews, and portfolios of your past work—to emphasize those strengths to the admissions staff.

3

REACHING OUT
to
TRANSFER STUDENTS

COLLEGE OFFICIALS SAY THEIR GOAL IS TO MAKE

the transfer recruitment process go as smoothly as possible for potential applicants, better enabling them to reach their dreams and desires. With roughly
4,000 two-year and four-year colleges in the United States and Canada, there
are a host of ways to recruit transfer students.

RECRUITMENT TECHNIQUES

In their quest for qualified transfers, colleges reach out to students through visits,
tours, mailings, alumni recommendations, and other recruitment methods. Here
are some of the most common ways they try to attract transfers.

COMMUNITY COLLEGE VISITS

"Our most successful method is the community college visit," says Teresa Mauk,
the admissions director at Texas Woman's University. This includes placing admissions counselors at tables and holding appointments there with potential transfer
students. Each spring, faculty members join an admissions counselor on each
community or junior college visit. Professors are invited based on the major interests of students at those two-year campuses.

Admissions counselors may visit on their own schedule, perhaps staffing a
booth at the student union or other popular spot on campus. Or they may participate in a college fair with their counterparts from other four-year institutions.

Either way, admissions counselors may bring brochures, catalogs, and other
printed material, show videos, and answer individual questions about the application process, fields of study, financial aid, and transferability of course credits.
Current students who are alumni of the two-year school they're visiting may
accompany them. In some instances, admissions counselors help prospective
transfer students fill out applications on the spot.

Some schools are selective in choosing which community colleges to visit. For
example, André Phillips, the transfer coordinator at the highly selective University
of Chicago (Illinois), visits only a handful of local community colleges, typically to
talk with students in special honors college programs there.

TRANSFER DAYS

To show what they have to offer, many colleges conduct transfer days in which a large number of prospective applicants tour the campus, meet with admissions and other staff, attend presentations on academic and nonacademic opportunities, and attend classes.

The University of Washington is among those hosting transfer days in which community and junior college students are invited to visit campus. The dean of student development services at Seattle Central Community College told the *Chronicle of Higher Education* that such events are crucial to encourage her students to transfer in light of the great differences between her school's small urban setting and the sprawling university campus: "It's culture shock. If they could just find their way around, it would help."

Most transfer days are open to all prospective transfers, but some colleges also schedule targeted transfer days. Suffolk University (Massachusetts), for example, hosts specialized open houses such as those aimed at transfers interested in business careers or arts and design careers.

Who will be at a transfer day? Expect faculty members, admissions and financial aid staff, representatives of the athletics department and extracurricular groups, as well as current students who are, themselves, transfers. Facilities, including residence halls and class buildings, are open, and guided tours are generally available. Frequently the college will provide lunch or snacks.

STUDENT RECRUITERS

These students—think of them as "ambassadors"—are undergrads who can make effective peer-level appeals to would-be transfer students. You might meet them at a college fair, during your campus visit, or during their visit to yours.

BRINGING COMMUNITY COLLEGE OFFICIALS TO CAMPUS

The State University of New York at Oswego hosts "transfer and transition" programs that bring administrators and faculty from two-year schools to campus to see what the university has to offer to transfer students. In turn, the community or junior college officials can more knowledgeably answer questions and talk up the school among their own students.

DIRECT MAIL

Some colleges send solicitations to prospective transfers, such as those scheduled to graduate from nearby community colleges. They also respond to phone, mail, and e-mail requests for printed information such as recruitment brochures, applications, and financial aid forms.

CD-ROMS

Not surprisingly in our high-tech times, colleges are looking for spiced-up ways to recruit transfer students and freshmen. A typical CD features audio and video clips, animation, and a soundtrack, as well as the usual information about academic departments, campus life, degree programs, resources, and links to the college's Web pages.

WEB SITES

The Internet is an increasingly potent and accessible recruitment device. A college Web site can provide detailed information on application and financial aid processes, available majors and courses, extracurricular opportunities, class schedules, campus maps, and even the applications themselves. Many Web sites include a virtual tour of campus high points, links to individual departments and programs, faculty biographies, course descriptions, and a means to ask questions quickly by e-mail.

A growing number of colleges allow you to apply online as well. Applicants provide a credit card number to cover the application fee.

COLLEGE FAIRS

College fairs are presented by multiple colleges and are open to both potential transfer and freshman applicants. They're generally held either at a high school or

"The primary goal of recruitment programs and activities is to influence the behavior of prospective students, their parents, and significant others in the college admissions process."

—Joyce E. Smith in "Recruitment: Student Outreach Strategies" in *Handbook for the College Admissions Process* (Greenwood Press, latest edition)

at a conference or convention center. Typically, each participating two-year or four-year institution has a table or booth with recruitment material, displays, catalogs, and applications. Many show a promotional video, and each has at least one representative to answer questions about admissions, financial aid, academics, credit transfers, housing, and campus life.

ALUMNI

If you're now a community or junior college student, you may hear from alumni who previously transferred to your target school. They're likely to be enthusiastic about their choice and can offer advice and firsthand information on the transition process, and on academic and lifestyle adjustments.

ACADEMIC DEPARTMENTS

Some academic departments get actively involved in the recruitment process. They may send faculty members to transfer college fairs, make professors available to interview prospective students, and review portfolios and audition tapes. They may receive lists of prospective majors from the admissions office to contact, and they may refer potential transfer students in their field to the admissions staff.

ATHLETES AND COACHES

If you're interested in playing intercollegiate sports at your target school, current team members and coaches may contact you as part of the college's recruitment efforts. Don't be afraid to ask them about your chances of making the team and playing if the college accepts you, services to help you balance sports and studying, and the availability of athletic scholarships for transfer students.

SPECIAL INCENTIVES

Given the competition for students, some colleges have become innovative in the quest for qualified transfer applicants. William Woods University (Missouri) offers new transfers a $5,000 tuition discount if they sign and fulfill an agreement to join campus organizations, participate in student government, or attend campus events, including athletic events. The college's LEAD (Leading, Educating, Achieving, Developing) Award Program sets out the minimum participation requirements, and the tuition breaks can be renewed from year to year.

FOLLOW-UP

The recruitment process may not end with your acceptance. At Michigan State University, for example, associate admissions director Thomas Hoiles says, "In an effort to enroll the most diversely rich transfer class, a number of . . . activities take place to help assure that students of color and out-of-state and international students actually enroll once admitted. These efforts include special letter-writing and telephone contacts by Office of Admissions and Scholarships staff and, in some cases, by academic units."

RECRUITERS

As knowledgeable and friendly as they may be, college admissions officers and recruiters owe their primary loyalty to their employers—the colleges—and not to prospective transfer students like yourself. They may be sincere and empathetic, but they operate in a competitive world, a marketplace where you are both a customer and a product. Given your experience already at one college (or more than one), don't be reluctant to inquire about sensitive issues or to press them further if you feel their answers aren't complete, clear, or frank. You're the one being solicited to make a significant commitment of time, money, and energy at the college, so regard yourself as an informed and astute consumer embarking on a potentially lucrative—or potentially costly—lifetime investment.

At the same time, don't underestimate the ability of admissions professionals to help you find out whether their college is a good fit. As the former assistant director of admissions at a private liberal arts college explains, "We made every effort to help students find the school that was right for them. It wasn't wise—or time-effective—to recruit 'bodies,' only to have them leave after a year."

QUESTIONS FOR PROSPECTIVE STUDENT-ATHLETES TO ASK

WHAT POSITIONS WILL I PLAY ON YOUR TEAM?

- It's not always obvious.
- Most coaches want to be flexible so that you are not disappointed.

DESCRIBE THE OTHER PLAYERS COMPETING AT THE SAME POSITION.

- If there is a former high-school all-American at that position, you may want to take that into consideration.
- This will give you clues as to what year you might be a starter.

CAN I "REDSHIRT" MY FIRST YEAR?

- Find out how common it is to redshirt and how that will affect graduation.
- Does the school redshirt you if you are injured?

WHAT ARE THE PHYSICAL REQUIREMENTS EACH YEAR?

- Philosophies of strength and conditioning vary by institution.
- You may be required to maintain a certain weight.

HOW WOULD YOU BEST DESCRIBE YOUR COACHING STYLE?

- Every coach has a particular style that involves different motivational techniques and discipline.
- You need to know if a coach's teaching style does not match your learning style.

WHAT IS THE GAME PLAN?

- For team sports, find out what kind of offense and defense is employed.
- For individual sports, find out how you are seeded and how to qualify for conference and national championships.

WHEN DOES THE HEAD COACH'S CONTRACT END?

- Don't make any assumptions about how long a coach will be at a school.
- If the coach is losing and the contract ends in two years, you may have a new coach.

DESCRIBE THE PREFERRED, INVITED, AND UNINVITED WALK-ON SITUATION. HOW MANY MAKE IT, COMPETE, AND EARN A SCHOLARSHIP?

- Different teams treat walk-ons differently.

—National College Athletic Association Student–Athlete Advisory Committee

4

SCOPE OUT
the
COLLEGES

targeting for a transfer. In some instances, a casual encounter through the cata-log or Web site, or a brief discussion with a couple of past and present students will be enough to scratch it off your list. In other situations, a first glimpse—actual or virtual—will pique your interest to delve deeper. The aim is to learn as much as possible and as soon as possible to realistically assess whether it will be suitable—academically, socially, and financially.

André Phillips, the associate director of admissions and the transfer coordinator at the University of Chicago (Illinois), advises would-be transfer students to "develop a good understanding of the schools to which they wish to transfer. Learn not just about what majors and programs are offered, but know something about the mission of the institution. Also, be able to articulate what they hope to accomplish during their time of study."

Wesleyan University (Connecticut) student Antonio Guerra, who transferred from a school in Rhode Island, suggests, "Make sure you know the school will be a better fit than your current school. Know that there are current transfer students there and talk to them about their experience."

THE COLLEGE

It's impossible to generalize or stereotype about colleges when there are literally thousands of institutions of higher learning in the United States and Canada. As a result, would-be transfer students owe it to their own futures to carefully examine a wide array of characteristics. Some are easy to check, including enrollment levels, acceptance rates for transfer applicants, and expenses. Others factors are subtler to pinpoint or describe, such as academic atmosphere and student demo-graphics. Ask around for different opinions. Because the choice of a college is such a personal decision, transfer applicants don't all give the same weight to each attribute of a target school—one factor may matter much more to you than to your friend.

WHAT TYPE OF COLLEGE IS IT?

How do you describe a college? One set of criteria involves the type of degree programs. A two-year community or junior college (even if the words "community" or "junior" aren't part of its name) awards associate's degrees and certificates, while a four-year institution grants bachelor's and sometimes graduate degrees. If you're finishing an associate's degree and want to continue your formal education, you're looking at four-year colleges—although some community colleges now award four-year degrees.

Governance is a second principal criteria area. Public institutions can be run by federal (as the military academies are), state, provincial, or local governments. Private colleges can operate as nonprofit entities or be operated by for-profit—so-called "proprietary"—corporations. In addition, a private college can be independent or it may have a formal affiliation, often with a religious denomination.

The form of governance has economic ramifications too. As a general rule, public institutions are less expensive than their private counterparts, particularly for in-state or in-district residents—because they get financial support from taxes—and that's a frequent motivating factor behind a transfer student's selection of target schools.

Academic thrust provides a third set of criteria. Is the college's focus narrow—such as music, studio arts, business, religion, or engineering? Many students who transfer from such schools say they prefer a wider array of programs and majors. On the other hand, students who are firmly committed to a career in one of those fields may decide that they'd benefit from exactly that type of tight focus.

Postgraduation plans offer yet a fourth set of criteria if you intend to attend graduate and professional school. You may have a better chance of winning acceptance to a program within the same university, although some graduate programs do prefer qualified applicants who earned their bachelor's degree elsewhere. In addition to the possibility of preferential admission, attending the same university offers several other advantages: a chance for you to take some graduate or professional-level courses as a senior, a chance to meet faculty in advance and possibly line up an assistantship or research opportunity, and a smoother transition after you finish your bachelor's degree.

You may, however, want to transfer. You already have experience with at least one type of school and might feel comfortable at another one of a similar type. Or you might prefer a dramatic change.

PHILOSOPHY AND MISSION

All colleges share certain goals such as spurring academic excellence, preparing students for future careers or advanced studies, encouraging analytical thinking, and developing life skills. Some also espouse a better-defined philosophy behind their mission, an overarching purpose rooted in intellectual, religious, or moral values. That philosophy may shape the courses required or offered, and it may require community service or compulsory attendance for faculty and students at daily religious services.

A religious affiliation does not automatically equate with a pervasive religious or denominational atmosphere. Students at some colleges with such affiliations find little practical difference compared with avowedly secular institutions. At other colleges, though, religious ties are reflected in the curriculum, graduation requirements, compulsory participation in worship, selection of faculty, roster of majors, nature of extracurricular groups and social activities, political orientation, diversity of students, and codes of conduct. At the same time, such institutions may cost less due to subsidies from their denomination or donors.

Be aware that an institutional philosophy may affect freedom of speech and freedom of thought for faculty and students. Some impose codes of conduct that go so far as to regulate whom students may date or even whether they may be married. Virginia Military Institute requires cadets to remain unmarried throughout their time there, for example.

"Don't be afraid to check out MANY schools—just because someone else tells you it is a good school, your perception may be different. Make sure that YOU feel like it's a good fit for you."

—JoLynne Oleson, director of testing and career services,
Cowley County Community College (Kansas)

A SAMPLING OF COLLEGE MISSION STATEMENTS

- *Earlham College (Indiana):* "It's an experience rooted in the Quaker values of tolerance, equality, justice, respect, and collaboration. It's an unending desire to see the world differently and to bring about change when necessary."

- *Mercy College (New York):* "Mercy encourages self-discovery and personal and social responsibility in a supportive learning environment in which students are challenged to live a life enhanced by the spirit of inquiry. The college encourages students to appreciate the natural and artistic realms; to grasp the complexity of moral issues; to recognize the significance of technologies; and to understand human differences in culture, gender, and race."

- *Brandeis University (Massachusetts):* "Brandeis is a community of scholars and students united by their commitment to the pursuit of knowledge and its transmission from generation to generation. As a research university, Brandeis is dedicated to the advancement of the humanities, arts, social, natural, and physical sciences. As a liberal arts college, Brandeis affirms the importance of a broad and critical education in enriching the lives of students and preparing them for full participation in a changing society, capable of promoting their own welfare, yet remaining deeply concerned about the welfare of others. The university that carries the name of the Supreme Court justice who stood for the rights of individuals must be distinguished by academic excellence, by truth pursued wherever it may lead, and by awareness of the power and responsibilities that come with knowledge.

- *Gustavus Adolphus College (Minnesota):* "The college aspires to be a community of persons from diverse backgrounds who respect and affirm the dignity of all people. It is a community where a mature understanding of the Christian faith and lives of service are nurtured and students are encouraged to work toward a just and peaceful world."

- *Friends University (Kansas):* "Honesty, sincerity, integrity, faith, and love are encouraged as necessary qualities of Christian character."
- *University of Dayton (Ohio):* "As Catholic, the university commits itself to a distinctive vision of learning and scholarship that includes: a common search for truth based on the belief that truth can be more fully known and is ultimately one; a respect for the dignity of each human person created in the image and likeness of God; and an appreciation that God is manifested sacramentally through creation and the ordinary things in life."
- *Virginia Military Institute:* "Providing an education within the framework of military discipline, VMI strives to educate the citizen-soldier for leadership roles in society, individual professions, and the military in times of national need."
- *Macalester College (Minnesota):* "We believe that education is a fundamentally transforming experience. As a community of learners, the possibilities for this personal, social, and intellectual transformation extend to us all. We affirm the importance of the intellectual growth of the students, staff, and faculty through individual and collaborative endeavor. We believe that this can best be achieved through an environment that values the diverse cultures of our world and recognizes our responsibility to provide a supportive and respectful environment for students, staff, and faculty of all cultures and backgrounds."

Philosophy also encompasses a college's approach to student independence. At one end of the spectrum, that's reflected in a lengthy list of required courses and an emphasis on traditional academic disciplines. At the opposite end are schools that push students to design, develop, and follow their own plan of studies, frequently without regard to traditional categories of majors.

When you chose your current college, its articulated philosophy—or lack of one—may not have been a principal factor in your decision. But now you're older and have more experience under your belt, so a college's set of principles may encourage or discourage you from applying there.

You'll generally find mission statements or statements of philosophy in college catalogs or on their Web sites. Some statements are highly detailed. At Grambling State University (Louisiana), the "statement of institutional mission and philosophy" covers equal access to higher education, opportunities for intellectual development, generation of new knowledge through research, service to the community, appreciation for diverse cultures, opportunities to use information technologies, and preservation of African-American heritage. The statement of Oglala Lakota College (South Dakota) discusses tribal, cultural, academic, and community missions.

Go beyond formal mission statements to get a sense of a school's vision and self-identity. Sometimes, all it takes is a phrase or short sentence to signal how an institution (if not its students) thinks of itself. Rhode Island School of Design characterizes itself as "a vibrant community of artists and designers," for instance, and Michigan State University labels itself as the nation's "pioneer land grant college."

The catalog, Web site, or recruitment material may provide other insights. The Antioch College (Ohio) Web site asks prospective students:

> Do you sometimes feel alone, at odds with the crowd? Does it make you angry when a race or a gender or a culture or a lifestyle is ridiculed or, worse, repressed? Do you admire character more than charisma? Does the phrase "That's the way things have always been done" make your blood boil? Do you want to learn about what most interests you? Do you want to combine study with "real world" experiences? Do you want to build a dynamic and diverse community? Do you want to be yourself? Do you want your voice to be heard?

Finally, many college Web sites have links to campus newspapers so you can get a student perspective on events.

SIZE

Some of us relish the bustle of crowds. Others prefer the intimacy of small groups. Size is a matter of comfort, and that varies according to individual personalities, living styles, and learning styles. So too with evaluating colleges. The size of the student body can determine how comfortable you'll feel.

STUDENT BODY

How big is the student body? Size counts in two ways: overall enrollment and class size.

First, what's the overall enrollment? There are colleges with fewer than five hundred full-time students and, at the other end of the spectrum, mega-campuses with more than forty thousand students, including the University of Texas at Austin, Ohio State University at Columbus, University of Minnesota–Twin Cities, and Michigan State University.

Size brings advantages and disadvantages, and it's a frequently cited reason for transferring.

You're more apt to know faculty and fellow students well on a smaller campus, and there will be more chances to hold leadership positions in organizations and win a spot on intercollegiate or intramural teams. Classes will be more intimate and you can expect more individualized attention. However, you'll probably have fewer majors and courses to choose from at a school of five thousand than a school of fifteen thousand. There may be less privacy as well if you feel that everybody knows your personal business.

On the other hand, the larger the school, the more varied the course offerings, the more diverse the faculty and students, the more available the specialized programs and research options, and the more eclectic the extracurricular opportunities. At the same time, you may feel lost in the crowds and unrecognized by your professors. You also may feel nobody cares—or even notices—how well you do or how you cope with problems and challenges, both personal and academic.

Second, overall size affects class size. That may be less of a problem for you as a transfer student who has already completed lower-level classes, such as introductory psychology, sociology, mass media, economics, political science, chemistry, or history courses that pack two hundred students into a lecture hall. No matter how large the new school and depending on your major, it's possible to craft a schedule dominated by small classes such as seminars, workshops, and laboratory courses. In addition, you can take the initiative to get involved, make yourself known to the professors, and avoid feeling lost among the masses.

As a transfer student, your current school provides a benchmark for comparison. Ask yourself: How well or poorly do I respond to its size? What would I get from a significantly larger or smaller college that I don't get where I am now? How assertive am I in meeting new people and jumping into social opportunities? How high a personal profile do I want to maintain?

CAMPUS

How big is the campus? Some colleges fit into a compact area—maybe a block or less in size that accommodates all the buildings and facilities. Others sprawl over thousands of acres, with lots of green space. Most fall somewhere in between.

If you want an easy, walkable campus, don't choose one that seems to stretch forever and requires long hikes or bus rides to get from class to class or between the residence halls, academic buildings, library, and athletic facilities. But if you like a sense of spaciousness and openness, you may feel restricted and hemmed in if the buildings are cheek by jowl.

LOCATION

What part of the United States or Canada do you want to be in, and in what type of community and setting?

No college is an island. Your assessment should include the advantages and liabilities of the nearby communities, including prospects for off-campus jobs. Explore the area by car, foot, or public transportation.

Do you enjoy the energy and excitement of big cities? See if there are professional theaters, clubs, professional sports teams, and other attractions nearby. Consider negatives too, such as traffic, crime, and higher living costs.

You may be most comfortable in a smaller city or rural area with ready access to outdoor activities such as canoeing, skiing, and bicycling. In a small community, the college itself is more apt to be the center of social life and recreation. However, services and part-time jobs may be more limited there.

Regardless of the location, look at the immediate neighborhood around campus. Can you walk quickly and safely to bookstores, fast-food restaurants, auto repair shops, supermarkets, and movie theaters?

For many transfer students, distance from family and hometowns is a decisive consideration. You may want to move far away, especially if you're now living with your parents and commuting. Or you may be lonely and want to be closer.

There is an option in which physical location is irrelevant: transferring to one of the small but growing number of "virtual" universities that have no campus and offer all their courses online. Jones International University (Colorado) was the first Web-based college to exist solely online and the first to be accredited. Others include Regents College (New York) and Western Governors University (Utah).

Is a virtual university a realistic alternative for you? Excelsior tells would-be applicants, "We have found that our students have the greatest chances for success if they can answer 'yes' to these questions:

• Do I plan ahead and am I organized and able to work independently?

• Have I earned college credits from a regionally accredited college or university?

• Am I motivated to complete my degree as soon as possible?"

Of course, you have more flexibility, but at the same time you don't get the human interaction with faculty and other students that is a valuable part of the college experience. It will take time to determine how well online degrees will be accepted among employers by admissions officers at graduate and professional schools.

"We recommend that students broaden their outlook—not limit themselves to one school."

—Charlotte Reall, senior admissions officer, Community College of Rhode Island

FACILITIES

Look into the quality of the facilities and the adequacy of such necessities as modern computers and whether there are enough of them to handle student demand. One Rhode Island community college student who was applying to transfer explained that "up-to-date equipment" and "good resources" were two of the three main features she looked for in the search for her target schools.

Ask about the number of publicly accessible computers on campus and whether computer labs and libraries are open late at night and on weekends. While the number of books in the libraries may be an indicator of a financial commitment to research, raw numbers don't tell how current the publications are and whether the college subscribes to the latest journals. Also find out the types of electronic databases the college makes accessible for student use. It's expensive to subscribe to some of those databases, but their availability may reduce a college's need to subscribe to traditional books, magazines, and newspapers.

Be alert because photos can be deceiving. Pictures in the recruitment material or catalog or on a college Web site are unlikely to show deteriorating buildings. Follow the advice in chapter 6, "Make the Campus Visit," and stop by campuses for the best sense of how well maintained the physical facilities are. Whether or not you're able to visit, contact a couple of current students or recent graduates to talk about the resources and facilities. It's better to hear horror stories—if there are any—about leaky roofs, fire traps, antiquated computers, broken-down desks, or shortages of athletic equipment ahead of time than after you're accepted and decide to attend.

COST

As you know, the costs of higher education traditionally rise faster than inflation, and you're looking at a multiyear commitment that could leave you deep—or deeper—in debt.

Sticker shock is especially likely to hit if you transfer from a public to a private institution, from a community or junior college to a four-year school, or both. Financial aid packages may help level things off if you're eligible.

The flip side is true if you transfer from a private to a public school, where tuition and fees are generally cheaper.

If you currently participate in a state-backed prepaid tuition or savings program, don't forget to take them into account when considering relative costs. In the eyes of most colleges, these programs generally reduce or eliminate the availability of need-based financial aid but shouldn't affect merit-based scholarships or grants. For more information on these programs, see chapter 12, "Financial Aid Opportunities for Transfer Students."

And if you're now staying at home but plan to live in a dorm, apartment, cooperative, or other off-campus housing, you may save on commuting expenses (gas, parking, public transportation) but are apt to pay a lot more for rent and utilities.

However, don't forget less easily measurable costs, such as the cost of time. For example, while living on campus may be more expensive in dollars based on the room rate and a mandatory meal plan, some students don't want to spend hours each week planning meals, shopping, cooking, washing dishes, and cleaning the kitchen.

Money magazine annually evaluates college expenses and publishes a list of "best buys." This type of assessment may help you decide whether a more expensive school is "worth it" in terms of academic caliber and programs.

Another major source of financial sticker shock: If you've been working full-time while attending college part-time, you face a drop—perhaps a cataclysmic one— in your earnings if you become a full-time student when you transfer.

Only a few expenses will remain the same from college to college, such as textbooks and supplies. Other than that, carefully examine all these cost elements for each target school:

• Tuition

• Fees

• Housing

• Meals

• Mandatory insurance

- Commuting
- Travel home for weekends and vacations

Here are more things to consider:

- In-state residency for public institutions
- Cooperative arrangements that offer discounted tuition to out-of-state residents from participating provinces and states, generally in the same geographic region
- Policies that treat active-duty military members as in-state residents for tuition purposes while they're stationed in that state
- Financial incentives for children and spouses of alumni
- State and federal income tax credits
- Availability and amount of financial aid
- Access to Army, Air Force, or Navy Reserve Officers Training Corps (ROTC) programs with scholarships and stipends
- Prospects for part-time employment and prevailing pay rates
- Overall cost of living locally, including rent, utilities, and auto insurance

If you're a U.S. citizen or permanent resident transferring to a Canadian college, you may confront an additional tuition burden. Concordia University (Quebec), for example, charges the lowest tuition to Quebec residents, charges other Canadians more than twice as much, and charges international students roughly five times as much as those from Quebec.

U.S. citizens heading for Canada and Canadians transferring to the United States should always pay attention to the relative value of their dollars. At this point, the U.S. dollar is much stronger, making higher education more affordable for U.S. students who go north of the border and much more expensive for Canadians switching to colleges south of the border.

International students, including Canadians, who transfer to U.S. colleges should also plan carefully to meet expenses. As Princeton University (New Jersey) advises, "Immigration regulations and restrictions on off-campus employment in the United States make it imperative that overseas applicants know where to obtain funds (for example, family resources, government grants, or savings)." A

U.S. Cultural Affairs Office can provide information about financial aid and travel grants from the U.S. government and private foundations.

As you narrow the field of target schools, consider the average debt load of their graduating seniors—the amount of loans they owe when they receive their degrees. A *U.S. News & World Report* study found debt loads as high as $35,000 at private colleges and over $28,000 in the public sector. At the opposite end of the spectrum, the magazine reported that there are both public and private universities whose new graduates carry an average debt load below $5,000. Those figures are based on only those students who incur debt and exclude any loans their parents took out.

FINANCIAL STABILITY AND RESOURCES

It may be tough to pin down, but try to find out whether the college is financially stable or whether there are rumors it may cut back programs, eliminate satellite campuses, sharply hike tuition and fees, lay off faculty, merge with another institution, or even shut down. Don't think it can't happen, because even long-established institutions can be vulnerable to economic problems.

Even schools in the public sector quake when government appropriations fail to keep up with increased enrollment. Oregon's seventeen community colleges put thousands of applicants on waiting lists in 2000–2001 because they didn't have enough money to pay new instructors. An official of the Oregon Community College Association told the *Chronicle of Higher Education* that part-time students were most affected: "These are students who need one course to transfer on to universities, or students who need a course for training at their workplace."

If that happens *after* you enroll, you could find yourself in limbo with little or no advance notice and a sudden need to transfer again.

Another issue to be aware of is that not all public institutions get equal amounts of state aid on a per-student basis to help cover salaries, facilities, and equipment. In some states, there is an imbalance in resources because the legislature uses different formulas or faces different political considerations in deciding how much to allocate to each campus. In Michigan, for example, that situation

> **Two essential questions: How competitive or noncompetitive is the school in evaluating transfer students? What proportion of transfer applicants are accepted?**

creates an annual debate over state aid among the four-year campuses. In Mississippi, the stark inequity in aid between historically black state colleges and predominantly white campuses led to more than twenty-five years of litigation in a long-running civil rights dispute. Under a settlement, the state is obligated to provide additional money for financial aid, enhancement of academic programs, construction, and other purposes. Virtually all of this additional money is set aside for historically black colleges.

Why should those political issues matter to you? As you consider colleges to transfer to, their state funding can affect the number and caliber of academic and research programs, as well as the tuition, fees, and other expenses you'll pay. It can also affect class size and whether faculty are full time or part time.

ACCEPTANCE RATES

Top colleges, no matter how elite—even the Ivies, renowned liberal arts schools, and the most competitive engineering, fine arts, and technology schools—accept transfer students. At the same time, it's natural that those that are highly selective with high school seniors will be at least equally selective when evaluating transfer students as well. Does that mean you shouldn't set your sights high, even if you were rejected before? Not at all.

Be candid, and ask what effect, if any, a prior rejection will have on your chances now. It's important to remember you're not the same applicant you were a year or two or several years earlier. By now, you may have overcome the lack of focus and direction that marred your high school experience—and have the latest grades to show it. Your interview, portfolio or audition, recommendations, work or military experience, volunteer activities, test scores, and essays may combine to make you far more desirable today than on your first go-round. Your confidence level and maturity should be higher, as well as your sense of what you want to study and what you want to do with your higher education.

Ask where most transfer students come from. It's comparatively unusual for a student to move from one top-ranked, exclusive college to another. Instead, transfers are more likely to want to "move up" to a more prestigious or well-respected college than they attend now, or from a two-year to a four-year institution. In addition, admission may be easier for transfer applicants from other colleges within the same state system.

Harvard University (Massachusetts), for example, admits a "small number of transfer students who present a clearly defined academic need for transfer, supported by both a proven record of achievement at the college level and strong faculty recommendations." In one recent year, that equated to only 70 of more than 1,100 transfer candidates who were accepted at Harvard. Another highly competitive school, Brown University (Rhode Island), says, "In recent years, approximately 750 applicants annually have presented credentials for transfer application to Brown," and the university "expects to greet" about 100 of them as enrollees.

Williams College (Massachusetts) cautions: "Williams has a very limited number of places available for transfer candidates, and the number has been decreasing over the last several years"—from a high of 25 percent to below 10 percent. Stanford University (California) encourages only transfer applicants with a grade point average of at least 3.5 and SAT verbal and math scores of 650 to 800, then adds, "Even applicants within these ranges will face stiff competition in our selection process, so all applicants should be realistic about their chances for admission." At the University of Pittsburgh (Pennsylvania), only 862 of 2,984 transfer applicants made the cut in a recent year. And Vassar College (New York) says, "In general, about one-third of the students seeking admission as transfers are successful."

The number of spaces available for transfers may change from year to year, and may vary according to your proposed major or program. If you find yourself part of a larger-than-usual pool of qualified candidates, the college's normal cutoff standards may be higher than you expected. Even if the target school has some form of guaranteed admission program, the academic criteria for acceptance may change, depending on your discipline and the year you hope to transfer.

Similarly, a highly desirable college may choose not to accept any transfers for a particular semester or academic year. Virginia Polytechnic Institute and Princeton University (New Jersey) explain that the factors behind such a decision include the number of freshmen accepted, their retention rate, overall enrollment, the availability of classes, and classroom space.

Be realistic: Many if not most rejected transfer applicants can do the work at the schools they apply to. Don't lose heart, though. Michele Hernandez, a former admissions officer at Dartmouth College (New Hampshire) and author of *A Is for Admission: The Insider's Guide to Getting into the Ivy League and Other Top Colleges,* (Warner Books, latest edition) explains that top-ranked schools seek diversity among transfer applicants. She writes, "The highly selective colleges try not to just accept students from other highly selective colleges because they'd end up with a pretty boring transfer group. Instead, students come from around the country and from many lesser-known, lower-profile colleges." For example, one year Dartmouth accepted transfers from colleges as varied as Ohio State University, Broward Community College (Florida), Santa Monica College (California), University of Colorado, Rockland Community College (New York), and Whitman College (Washington), among others.

In addition, the absolute number of transfer students who enroll each year tells only part of the story. So does the relationship between that number and the total undergraduate student body. Don't stop there, though. Those numbers suggest other questions for you to ask the admissions staff:

- How eager and aggressive is the school in recruiting potential transfer students?
- What proportion of those accepted actually enrolls?
- If transfer students account for an unusually high percentage of the student body, does that indicate a low retention rate that creates so many spots? If so, why?

Pay attention to special arrangements that pretty much guarantee acceptance if you start at the right community college and know where you want to transfer when you finish your two-year degree. For example, the University of Massachusetts at Lowell takes part in a joint admissions program with fifteen community colleges in the state. Here's how it works: "Students selecting Lowell are conditionally accepted at the same time they enroll in the community college of their choice. If a joint admissions student completes a designated associate's degree with a GPA of 3.0 or better, he or she is also entitled to a one-third reduction of in-state tuition."

STUDENTS WITH DISABILITIES

If you have a disability that requires accommodation, be sure that facilities—from class buildings to dorms to athletic centers—where you intend to transfer are accessible. While federal and state laws set minimum standards for accessibility, not all campuses fully meet those standards yet, and some older buildings are especially difficult to bring into compliance.

If you have impaired vision or hearing, will the college provide you with interpreters and note takers who can attend classes with you? If you have a learning disability, will instructors accommodate your need for alternative testing methods or times? Will the college provide tutors and study skills assistance? Is enough handicapped parking available near residence halls, classrooms, athletic and health facilities, the library, and other buildings? Is there priority registration? On the technology front, does the college have computers that can scan textbooks and other reading assignments, then read them aloud to you?

Some colleges have learning diagnostic clinics or programs that provide academic support for students with such disabilities as dyslexia or attention deficit disorder (ADD) or attention deficit hyperactivity disorder (ADHD). Does your target school offer such services, and is there a fee for using them?

Incidentally, there is one college in the United States exclusively for students with learning disabilities or ADHD, the two-year Landmark College (Vermont). It claims that it provides ambitious and motivated students "with the skills needed for academic success. Our programs are designed exclusively to meet the needs of these students and are tailored to meet the specific needs and goals of each individual student. Because our student-faculty ratio is three to one, every Landmark student receives personalized instruction and attention. All students are provided with intense one-on-one tutorials which help them identify their individual learning styles. Students develop the critical language and study skills that will allow them to work within the expectations of academia and the workforce."

WHO GOES THERE?

While the size of the student body—both undergrad and grad—may be important to you, it's also important to learn the characteristics and makeup of the student body at any college you're considering. That will help you assess how well you think you'll fit in, the diversity and geographic roots of the students you'll meet, and the types of cultural and extracurricular opportunities available. Some colleges pride themselves on the diversity of their student body.

Don't succumb to stereotypes—party school, geek school, preppy school, racist school, jock school. California Institute of Technology, for example, says it faces four common misperceptions: you must be a genius to be admitted, students lack time for a social life, graduates emerge as "pretty narrow" people, and its students are "obsessively studious, socially awkward, calculator-toting nerds." Colleges may find it a challenge to overcome such stereotypes, but beyond their protestations, it's incumbent on you to look at who goes there.

Key student population indicators include:

MALE-FEMALE RATIO

The number of single-gender colleges has shrunk, but the proportion of men to women at coeducational institutions varies, as does the proportion within departments. Overall nationally, women today account for a significant majority of college students. Their enrollment in many traditionally male fields such as business has increased dramatically, although their gains have been smaller in some other historically male majors such as the physical sciences and engineering. At the same time, the proportion of men has risen in the predominantly female fields of nursing, home economics, and elementary education.

For some students, a single-gender school is most comfortable. One such institution, Agnes Scott College (Georgia), says students at women's colleges participate more fully in and out of class, get more leadership opportunities, develop higher levels of self-esteem, and tend to hold higher positions in their careers. Hampden-Sydney College (Virginia) says it "has sustained its mission to form good men and good citizens in an atmosphere of sound learning" since 1776. If you prefer to attend an all-men's or all-women's school, many participate in social and recreational activities, as well as consortia or course-sharing relationships, with nearby colleges, either coeducational or for students of the opposite gender. The all-women's Mount Holyoke College and Smith College participate in Five Colleges, Inc., a consortium with three coeducational institutions in Massachusetts: Amherst College, the University of Massachusetts at Amherst, and Hampshire College. All-male St. John's University and all-female College of St. Benedict in Minnesota call themselves "partners in liberal arts education, providing students the opportunity to benefit from the distinctions of not one, but two, nationally recognized Catholic undergraduate colleges."

RACIAL, ETHNIC, AND RELIGIOUS BREAKDOWN

Beyond percentages, here are several things to consider: First, some campuses run internationally recognized ethnic studies programs, such as Scottish studies at Alma College (Michigan) and Irish studies at Southern Illinois University. Second, many schools offer interdisciplinary majors in ethnic, racial, or religious studies. Third, the United States has a strong tradition of historically black colleges and universities, predominantly but not exclusively in the South. And fourth, even among denomination-affiliated colleges, there's wide variation in the proportion of adherents to that religion. Some denominational colleges require attendance at religious services or a minimum number of religion-related courses.

PROPORTION OF TRANSFER STUDENTS

As we've explained, many colleges seriously recruit transfer students. Like you, they are frequently more mature and experienced than freshly minted high school grads and are more apt to actively participate in class discussions and group projects.

PROPORTION OF IN-STATE VERSUS OUT-OF-STATE STUDENTS

The wider the geographical locations students come from, the greater the potential diversity in their backgrounds and interests. Of course, the mix also reflects the fact that public institutions charge lower tuition to in-state residents and, sometimes, to residents of adjoining states. At the same time, remember that highly rated public institutions may set tougher admissions standards for out-of-state transfers than for applicants from their home state. For students there, that may affect placement opportunities for internships and cooperative work assignments, access to job recruiters, and even the availability of sharing rides back home for holidays and vacations.

PROPORTION OF INTERNATIONAL STUDENTS

Foreign students bring different ways of thinking to campus, along with different traditions, languages, backgrounds, and life experiences. The more foreign students there are on campus, the greater your chance to become exposed to those enriching differences. Remember, if you're a U.S. citizen or legal resident who transfers to a Canadian institution, you'll be an international student there. Similarly, Canadian citizens transferring to U.S. colleges are regarded as international students too.

PROPORTION OF UNDERGRADS TO GRADS

Numbers don't tell the full story here either, but the faculty in some departments put a greater emphasis on their graduate students than on their undergrads. That could make it tougher to develop close relationships with some professors. On the other hand, the presence of graduate students in a department—and even in some of your own advanced undergrad courses—may enrich the quality of learning and research opportunities. A strong graduate program also can enhance the reputation of your new college and academic department.

MOST COMMON ACADEMIC INTERESTS

What fields of study draw the most students? A technology-oriented or engineering-oriented college will offer English and social sciences courses, but those generally receive fewer resources than physics, chemical engineering, math, or computer science. Ask for a breakdown of academic interests. Although the proportions may shift from year to year, Brown's breakdown shows about 36 percent of its undergrads interested in sciences and math, 10 percent in engineering, 25 percent in humanities, 15 percent in social sciences, and the rest undecided.

MOST POPULAR MAJORS

Sure, a department may be strong, but its popularity may make it harder to be admitted to that major, may contribute to larger-than-preferred class size, and may make it more difficult to meet with academic advisors and faculty. Classes with limited enrollment, such as senior seminars and lab courses, may fill quickly, closing you out of them. However, schools may also support popular majors financially, so that those majors remain accessible and attractive.

AVERAGE AGE OF UNDERGRADS

Students between twenty-five and thirty-four represent the fastest-growing sector of campus populations nationally. Without stereotyping, older students tend to be better organized, more diligent, and more committed than their younger counterparts. Again, that may add to the quality of classroom discussions and the caliber of work. On the other hand, many older students have family or job commitments as well as classes, making them less likely to get involved in extracurricular activities and organizations.

COMMUTERS VERSUS ON-CAMPUS RESIDENTS

Does campus empty when classes end? Commuters frequently head home when they're done for the day, or spend their evenings in the library when they do hang around. That could be reflected in a less lively social atmosphere on campus at night and on weekends.

PROPORTION OF PART-TIME STUDENTS

Part-time students generally don't get as involved in groups and after-hours activities as full timers. Most work, have child-raising responsibilities, or both. As a result, you won't have as much of an opportunity to get to know them outside of class.

AVERAGE ENTERING SAT OR ACT SCORE

Test scores do more than help admissions officers choose among a pool of applicants. From your vantage point as a prospective transfer student, they serve as one measure of the academic caliber of the student body.

PROPORTION OF TRANSFER STUDENTS

How many transfer applicants enroll in a typical year and how many under-grads are there? The range is great, as this sample from a variety of colleges in one recent year shows:

COLLEGE	TRANSFER STUDENTS ENROLLED	FULL-TIME UNDERGRADS
Yale University (Connecticut)	23	5,300
Western Maryland College	56	1,600
Jackson State University (Mississippi)	461	4,300
West Point (New York)	166	4,200
University of California at Los Angeles	2,249	25,000
Vanderbilt University (Tennessee)	69	5,700
University of Tampa (Florida)	354	2,300
Willamette University (Oregon)	354	1,600
Atlanta College of Art (Georgia)	68	400
University of Wisconsin at Parkside	400	2,700

Particularly if you plan to transfer to a different state, you'll see overall variations among student bodies that may affect your decision of where to go. A study by the nonpartisan National Center for Public Policy in Higher Education, which has offices in Washington D.C., and San Jose, California, found that people in some states have a much higher chance of going to college than others. While 38 percent of eighteen- to twenty-four-year-olds in California are in college, only 20 percent are in Nevada. Meanwhile in Delaware, 6.3 percent of twenty-five- to forty-four-year-olds are enrolled part-time in college-level education, contrasted with 1.8 percent in Montana. The study, "Measuring Up 2000," said there are sharp financial disparities as well, because people in some states spend a larger chunk of their income to attend. In Illinois, tuition minus financial aid at public four-year schools takes about 24 percent of family income, much lower than the 36 percent figure for New York. Students in some states borrow more heavily too. For instance, the per-student average for all types of student loans in Massachusetts is $4,719 a year, but only $3,168 in Minnesota. Finally, the proportion of students who complete a bachelor's degree within five years stretches from a low of 28 percent in Louisiana to a 68 percent high in Vermont.

THE SERVICES

College life involves plenty more than classes and faculty, yet would-be transfer students often pay too little advance attention to the organizations and support services that enrich a campus. From sports to residence halls, from safety to health care, those services can make all the difference between a positive and a painful college experience.

EXTRACURRICULAR OPPORTUNITIES

Extracurricular opportunities are especially important during your first semester or two on a new campus because they provide an entrée to student life, a chance to meet other students, and an avenue to get to know the campus more intimately. Chapter 15, "Survive the Transition," discusses in detail how to get involved once you transfer.

What do you enjoy in your free time? And are those activities available on or near campus? Find out. Here are some of the most common categories of activities, some of which may not be available at your present school:

- Intramural athletics
- Sports facilities for personal use including ice rink, swimming pool, bowling alley, courts for tennis and racquet sports, running tracks, basketball courts, and fitness centers
- Student government
- Religious organizations

- Student theater, dance, film, and music performance groups
- Art gallery or campus museum that displays student work
- Fraternities and sororities, whether or not they offer housing
- Honor and leadership societies
- Volunteer service groups such as Big Brothers–Big Sisters and Habitat for Humanity and "alternative break" programs that help students spend their vacations on community service, either in the country or abroad
- Ethnic and cultural organizations
- Campus publications—newspaper, yearbook, literary magazine
- International student associations
- Campus service groups
- Political and public affairs groups, such as affiliates of the Democratic, Republican, and Green parties, or clubs interested in environmental issues, world peace, human rights, civil liberties, or poverty
- Student chapters of national career-related organizations in fields as diverse as chemical engineering, hospitality, horticulture, accounting, and public relations
- Broadcasting—campus radio, television, and cable stations

Don't merely rely on a laundry list of organizations and programs. Find out how active they are, whether they have faculty sponsors, how many students participate, and whether the college provides them with financial support.

INTERCOLLEGIATE ATHLETICS

Varsity sports are a big draw for many transfer students, both aspiring players and exuberant fans. If you want to play, find out what the team's requirements are, how you can try out, and what the odds are you'll make the team *and* get to play. It's also crucial to know what the time commitments will be for training and practice, how much time you'll spend traveling, and what academic standards you must maintain to remain eligible. Ask how past transfer students have acclimated to the team and talk with several of them, as well as with the coaches.

Does the school's mission or philosophy directly affect the athletic program, and how? Eastern Mennonite University (Virginia) tells prospective students up front that "Christian values are the foundation for all athletic activities, giving players a chance to integrate athletic skills with personal growth, academic excellence, wholesome attitudes and spiritual understanding."

If you want to participate in intercollegiate athletics, be sure to speak with your prospective coaches about National Collegiate Athletic Association (NCAA) or National Association of Intercollegiate Athletics (NAIA) eligibility rules. Each organization has a complex set of bylaws that dictate when transfer students can start competing on behalf of their new schools. You may face a "residence" period of up to a full academic year when you can practice with the team but not play or receive travel expenses. The applicable rules may differ, depending on whether you're coming from a two-year or a four-year school, whether you play at your current school, what division the college is placed in, and whether you were recruited or hope to be a walk-on. The bylaws set out procedures for exceptions.

A 1972 federal law known as Title IX prohibits discrimination on the basis of gender in educational opportunities at colleges that receive federally backed student loans, contracts, and research grants. That ban on discrimination applies to college athletics and has led to a dramatic change in the allocation of funds among men's and women's teams. Prospective students are entitled to review a college's latest report regarding its compliance with Title IX, prepared under the Federal Equity in Athletics Disclosure Act.

The U.S. General Accounting Office, an investigative arm of Congress, reported in "Gender Equity: Men's and Women's Participation in Higher Education" that the proportion of women taking part in intercollegiate sports at four-year institutions has increased under Title IX, and the gender gap between male and female participation rates has narrowed. Its study found that coeducational NCAA schools spend less on recruitment, operations, and coaching salaries per female than per male intercollegiate sports participant. But at the same time, the average per-participant expenditure for athletics-related scholarships is higher for women than for men.

The mix of intercollegiate sports offered by a school can change from year to year due to pressures from Title IX, budget considerations, and shifting student interests. Another General Accounting Office study ("Intercollegiate Athletics: Four-Year Colleges' Experiences Adding and Discontinuing Teams") that traced male and female participation reported an increase in the overall number of teams for each gender at NCAA and NAIA campuses between 1981 and 1999. For both genders, the most teams added were in soccer. Proportionately, there were significant increases in women's golf, water polo, and equestrian teams. For men, the largest proportionate increase was in equestrian teams, but there was growth in other sports from basketball to rowing.

However, many schools dropped teams over the same period, the government study showed. For women, gymnastics accounted for the largest net decrease in the number of teams, with losses in archery, field hockey, and fencing, among others. Wrestling saw the biggest decrease among men's teams, but there was also a net decline in football, swimming, ice hockey, and other sports.

If you hope to compete, make careful inquiries into whether your target school is discussing the elimination of your team or, conversely, adding a team in a sport you want to play.

HEALTH CARE

The availability of on-campus health services varies tremendously from school to school. Some operate medical, dental, and mental health clinics as well as a pharmacy. Others may offer nothing at all. Among colleges with clinics, policies vary on what services student fees pay for, what services are covered through private insurance, and what services you need to pay for from your own pocket. Health prevention services are important too. They include material about tobacco, drugs, alcohol, and other potentially addictive substances; HIV/AIDS; counseling and support groups; workshops and classroom presentations; and referrals.

If you have special health needs—for example, you need regular allergy shots—find out how each school will help you handle them.

See whether confidential mental health services are available, either with on-campus psychologists or psychiatrists or through an off-campus agency. Even if you don't use such services now, trauma, grief, depression, or other emotional crises can strike unexpectedly.

CHECKING OUT ON-CAMPUS HOUSING

If you want to live on campus, at least initially, check out the types of housing facilities offered.

• In a dorm or residence hall, are there private rooms, double rooms, suites?

• Are there on-campus apartments and, if so, are they available only to married couples and families?

• What condition is the housing in?

• Does everything seem safe and clean?

• `What kind of security is there to keep out unwanted people?

• Are there study and computer facilities?

• Is there enough parking nearby?

• Are you assured on-campus housing if that's what you want, especially if you transfer for the spring semester? Or are transfers placed at the end of the line, behind returning students and incoming freshmen?

Housing raises lifestyle and tolerance issues too.

• Is there a curfew?

• Are overnight guests allowed?

• Are the dorms all-male, all-female, coeducational, or a mix?

• Are there tobacco-free, alcohol-free, and drug-free dorms?

HOUSING

Research shows that students who live on campus interact more with other students, have more contact with faculty, do better academically, are more likely to graduate, become more involved in extracurricular activities, and report higher satisfaction with their undergrad experience. If you've never lived on campus, you may want to try it for your first semester or year as a transfer student. However, a residence hall or on-campus apartment may offer less privacy and more distractions than you're used to.

CHECKING OUT OFF-CAMPUS HOUSING

Off-campus living options range from fraternity and sorority houses to co-ops, from renting a room in somebody's house or renting a house or mobile home, to living with parents.

• What will it cost for rent compared to on-campus living?

• How wide is the selection?

• Will you need to buy or rent furniture and appliances, or are they provided?

• How close or how far will you be from campus, and will you get there by foot, bike, car, or public transportation?

• Is parking available?

• How safe is the neighborhood?

If you want to live off campus, make sure it's allowed. Marlboro College (Vermont) requires all new students—transfers as well as freshmen—to live on campus. Kent State University (Ohio) requires all students enrolled for at least nine credits to live in a residence hall and participate in the food plan until they attain junior standing or receive an exemption. Reasons for exemptions include a daily commute from a parent's home within a fifty-mile radius of campus or residence in a fraternity or sorority. Exemptions are also granted for married students, for single parents with primary child-rearing responsibilities, for active-duty military veterans, and for students who lived in college housing for at least four semesters.

Many campuses offer theme-based housing options. Those include dorms or parts of dorms with an ethnic or religious focus, or for honors students, or for students interested in a particular academic area such as French language and culture, natural sciences, or environmental studies. The University of Missouri at Columbia describes them as "living-learning communities," some of which are sponsored by academic departments.

PLACEMENT, JOBS, AND GRADUATE STUDIES

A satisfying and well-paid job? Graduate and professional school? Military or volunteer service? Whatever options you're considering when you complete your degree, find out how well each target college can help you get there.

Many colleges run placement and career-planning centers that draw recruiters to campus, critique résumés and cover letters, conduct mock interviews, provide career-related guidebooks and online reference material, and distribute career-related magazines. They may post job announcements, host career and job fairs, track the job placement rate of alumni, conduct interviewing workshops, and even advise students how to dress appropriately for a job interview. For students interested in working abroad, they may provide information on international internships, short-term work abroad programs, and on-campus interviews with companies and organizations that have foreign subsidiaries, offices, and operations. They may also keep sample résumés and cover letters on file.

Ask whether the placement center administers any of the standardized career-planning tests such as the Strong Interest Inventory and the Self-Directed Search to help match your interests to specific careers. There also may be specialized placement services for students of color; gay, bisexual, and lesbian students; students with disabilities; and international students. Be sure to ask.

If graduate or professional school appears to be in your future, see whether the college helps prep its students for admissions tests, conducts graduate and professional school fairs, collects catalogs, critiques applications, and sponsors on-campus interviews by admissions officers from other institutions.

If your target college uses a nontraditional grading system, ask how that affects graduate and professional school applications. At Sarah Lawrence College (New York), for example, instructors write reports about their students each semester, detailing achievements and shortfalls. The college says those evaluations are more useful than letter grades in assessing students' progress, but the college does keep letter grades on file for use on transcripts.

Many schools are proud of their placement rates and publish the results of periodic surveys of how their graduates fare. Robert Morris College

(Pennsylvania) publishes the average starting base salary of its alumni; the geographic distribution of their first jobs; the range and mean of entry-level salaries according to majors such as finance, communication, and sport management; and a roster of its top-twenty employers. The University of Michigan at Ann Arbor issues compensation surveys about its bachelor of business grads, with base salaries and total compensation arranged by region and industry, such as accounting, consulting, financial services, automotive, and telecommunication services. Southwest Missouri State University's transfer guide lists an array of prime jobs held by recent grads and prestigious graduate schools that recent alumni attend.

CHILD CARE AND PARENTING SERVICES

If you have young children, see whether day-care services are available on or near campus, as well as what they charge and whether there will be openings. Since many transfer students are older than the average "traditional" undergraduate, this is likely to be a particular concern. A college with an early childhood education or child development department may run its own day-care center or preschool facility as a teaching laboratory, providing convenient and reasonably priced supervision for your children.

Many colleges offer extensive support services for students who need to balance academic, family, and work commitments. They may run a resource center to help you find suitable child care, counseling, and financial assistance. A few provide special services such as care for sick children, emergency backup care, and free child care during the week before finals.

See if there's a support organization on campus for student-parents. These groups serve as information networks about child health and nutrition, jobs, financial aid, and free or inexpensive family activities in the area. They may hold meetings with guest speakers, create child-care or baby-sitting cooperatives, and put on social activities and events.

If you, your spouse, or your partner is pregnant, ask about programs for new parents, including workshops, counseling, prenatal medical screening, and support groups.

SOME POSTGRADUATE ISSUES TO EXPLORE

- What proportion of new grads go on to professional or graduate schools, and where?
- Which employers hire the largest number of new grads from the college?
- What's the range and mean of entry-level salaries of new grads, by major?
- In what geographic areas do most new grads find their first jobs?
- What percentage of students find jobs within six months of graduation, and what proportion of them relate to their majors?

OTHER SERVICES

With thousands of colleges in the United States and Canada, it's no surprise that the range of available services varies tremendously. Here are some other services you may encounter that are covered by your tuition and fees:

- Many colleges have support services or an office for gay, lesbian, bisexual, and transgendered students. They provide counseling, run workshops, and offer other forms of assistance.
- Some provide legal services to help students with off-campus problems such as landlord-tenant disputes. The lawyers and paralegals can help interpret and prepare legal documents, assist in negotiation, and give professional advice, although the staff may not represent you in court.
- Computer centers may assist you in designing your own Web site, offer training sessions on popular software packages, and sell computers, software, and accessories at a discount.
- Services for military veterans, including counseling and assistance on educational benefits may be available.

SECURITY

Regretfully, crime doesn't stop at the edge of campus. Stolen backpacks, burglarized dorms, rapes, and even an occasional murder may occur, committed by students and nonstudents. Quite wisely, more and more transfer students make security a prime concern when evaluating colleges, especially if they come from small, safe schools in small communities and are considering large urban campuses.

At most campuses, the reality is that some students under twenty-one drink and some students, regardless of age, use drugs. If that bothers you, ask about policies and counseling for abusers.

Federal law now requires colleges and universities to report crimes on their campuses. Those statistics are available on request from each college. Or you can find them electronically through the Internet from the U.S. Department of Education (Web address below), which tells users, "Campus security and safety is an important feature of postsecondary education. The department is committed to assisting schools in providing students nationwide a safe environment in which to learn and to keep students, parents and employees well informed about campus security." A 1998 amendment to the law now requires disclosure of statistics for crime in certain off-campus areas as well.

Federal law also requires colleges to have campus sexual assault policies, including assistance for victims in notifying police, and to disclose information about convicted registered sex offenders who are enrolled at or employed by colleges.

Go to the U.S. Department of Education's Office of Postsecondary Education Web site at **www.ope.ed.gov/security** for a form that allows you to check crime statistics for thousands of public and private institutions, including proprietary—for-profit—ones. The results cover reported criminal offenses, actual arrests, and college disciplinary actions. By filling in the blanks, you can search the database by a combination of variables: state, type of institution, name, instructional program, and even size of enrollment. For example, you can search all private not-for-profit four-year colleges with computer information programs and a student body of ten- to twenty-thousand in New England.

If you examine schools with on-campus housing, their figures will indicate how many reported offenses in each category (murder, assault, forcible sex crimes, arson, negligent manslaughter) took place in residence halls.

For more about safety issues, check out Security on Campus Inc., a national nonprofit organization committed to preventing campus violence and crime. Its Web site at **www.campussafety.org** includes links to crime statistics, updated information on campus crime legislation, and advice on personal safety, binge drinking, and related topics. It also monitors complaints against institutions that fail to properly report criminal incidents and arrests.

Don't let grapevine gossip and hearsay dictate where you'll transfer. Instead, take control of the decision by doing your homework into the many dimensions of life at each college you're considering. The truth is, nobody else—not a transfer counselor, not a friend, not an admissions officer—can handle this research responsibility as well as you can, and nobody else has as big a stake as you do in making the best informed decision possible.

5

SCOPE OUT
the
ACADEMICS

CAN YOU JUDGE A COLLEGE BY ITS REPUTATION?

Not entirely, although a school's reputation suggests the comparative regard with which higher education experts, employers, and others hold it.

Why does reputation matter? First, job recruiters and graduate school admissions officers consider it. Second, it may help justify (at least in your mind or your parents' minds) higher-than-average tuition. Third, it may add to the value the alumni network offers when you finish. Finally, it may attract donations and government and corporate grants that underwrite scholarships, high-tech facilities, and research projects.

Be careful, though:

• Don't be seduced by big names or stale legends of grandeur.

• Don't think that a college's reputation in one area—football, perhaps, or physics, or campus beauty—automatically reflects its overall caliber.

• Don't equate reputation with academic excellence and intellectual creativity.

On the other hand—and this is equally important—many colleges that are little known outside their state, province, or region may provide an equal or superior—and frequently less expensive—education and prepare you as well or better for the future than high-ticket, big-name schools.

Beyond gossip, "common knowledge," and a college's self-serving statements, how can you assess the reputation of a school, especially one located a long distance from where you live today? If you're at a community or junior college now, ask the transfer counselors or advisors for their evaluations and impressions. If you know any alumni of the target school, ask for specifics on how its reputation helped or hindered them.

Another way to investigate is by reading independent, comparative rankings. The accuracy and validity of these evaluations draw intense criticism and skepticism from some academic authorities, but they do provide guidance. They consider such factors as academic reputation, student selectivity, faculty resources, per-student spending, graduation and retention rates, and alumni financial support. Most of the information used to make the assessments comes from the colleges, and some of the rest from professional associations. Regardless of source, the data then goes through an analysis that involves subjectivity and judgment, not scientific preciseness.

Don't merely rely on the overall rankings. There's little difference between numbers one and two on a list, and the differences between numbers one and twenty-one may be insignificant or irrelevant to your individual interests or needs.

The more that information is broken down, the more useful it's apt to be. For example, the annual rankings by *U.S. News & World Report* magazine sort colleges into these types of categories, although the specific groupings may vary from year to year:

- Best national universities
- Best national liberal arts colleges
- Best regional universities (North, South, Midwest, West)
- Best regional liberal arts colleges (North, South, Midwest, West)

There can be other breakdowns as well. In rating business programs, *U.S. News & World Report* ranks such departments as accounting, entrepreneurship, management information systems, quantitative analysis, real estate, and marketing. Within its best engineering programs, the magazine ranks departments that include biomedical, electrical, mechanical, civil, and aerospace engineering. However, not all schools—and not all "good" schools—participate in the *U.S. News & World Report* study.

Recruitment information from individual colleges may highlight these kinds of favorable ratings, as well as ratings about safety or student retention. While self-promotions like these aren't inherently misleading, they may be incomplete. That's why you should examine a more complete evaluation from independent sources.

Finally, be honest with yourself about the degree of intellectual challenge you want, and don't assume that a college's top-flight reputation guarantees automatic stimulation. I believe that any student *can* be challenged at any college, but it's not inherent in a school's rankings or reputation. Writing about "intellectually disengaged" students in the *Chronicle of Higher Education*, Duke University (North Carolina) Professor Stuart Rojstaczer observed, "The hardest thing for students at Duke—and at most elite institutions, is getting in. Once admitted, a smart student can coast, drink far too much beer, and still maintain a B+ average. . . . There are problems with that niche. It's pleasant for the type of students we attract, but is making students comfortable what education is about?"

ACCREDITATION

Most two-year and four-year institutions are accredited, but check whether the program, department, or major you're considering is also accredited or approved by a national professional association. Although accreditation doesn't *guarantee* the quality of an academic department, its faculty, or courses, it's a significant indicator that the program and curriculum pass periodic muster after careful review by authorities in the field. Accreditation may also prove to be an asset later when you apply for a job, internship, graduate school, or professional school.

Aside from formal accreditation, colleges can receive approval of their programs and curricula from professional groups, including the American Chemical Society, American Dietetic Association, Council for Standards in Human Services Education, Council on Aviation Accreditation, Association of University Programs in Health Administration, and American Music Therapy Association.

However, some high-quality programs and departments choose not to be accredited or approved by a national association for a variety of reasons. Some dislike the restrictions that accreditation may impose on their curriculum and course offerings. Others feel the accreditation process is too time consuming for their faculty and administrators and not worth the effort.

WHO TEACHES THERE?

It's tough to gauge the collective caliber of a college's faculty, even on a department-by-department or major-by-major basis, as you know from the courses you've already taken. Does *caliber* include teaching style, degrees, research successes, availability to students, keeping up-to-date in their fields, motivational ability, awards received, and creative work published, performed, exhibited, or recorded?

Yes—all that and more.

SOME OF THE MOST COMMON ACCREDITED PROGRAMS

- *Accounting:* American Assembly of College Schools of Business–International Association for Management
- *Education:* National Council for Accreditation of Teacher Education
- *Engineering:* Accreditation Board for Engineering and Technology
- *Forestry:* Society of American Foresters
- *Interior design:* Foundation for Interior Design Education Research
- *Journalism and communications:* Accrediting Council for Education in Journalism and Mass Communication
- *Legal studies:* American Bar Association's Standing Committee on Legal Assistants
- *Music:* National Association of Schools of Music
- *Nursing:* Commission on Collegiate Nursing Education or National League for Nursing Accrediting Commission
- *Occupational therapy:* American Occupational Therapy Association's Accreditation Council for Occupational Therapy Education
- *Social work:* Council on Social Work Education
- *Sport and leisure studies:* American Association for Leisure and Recreation

Don't get seduced into looking at only one or two attributes—a single stellar or even popular professor does not make a major or a university. Each department is the sum of its teachers. And each college is the sum of its departments.

The Nobel laureate in economics, the Pulitzer Prize–winner in journalism, the National Book Award honoree in English, the astronomer who formerly served in the White House as the President's science advisor, and the former governor now teaching political science all look great in the catalog and on the college Web site. They add prestige to the institution and may help raise money and secure grants.

But do they regularly teach undergrads? How effectively do they teach? Do they connect intellectually with their students and convey a sense of excitement in their material? And on a practical level, are they available for office hours and appointments, or do they spend most of their time in research or off campus doing "more important" things?

Each professor is the sum of his or her achievements and failures, personality, interests, and energy levels. In addition, faculty members come and go, and the professors listed in this year's catalog may move, die, retire, or go on sabbatical leave before you show up for your first class or by the time you're ready for their advanced-level courses.

When it comes to faculty, here are some critical questions:

- What proportion of your classes will full-time faculty teach? Part-time or adjunct instructors? Graduate assistants? Many adjuncts are excellent teachers, both knowledgeable and inspirational, and if their "day" job relates to the course material, they can bring daily real-world experiences to class with them. Graduate teaching assistants may be skilled and polished instructors but many have little or no teaching experience yet—one reason they're in grad school. Is English the second or third language for many of the TAs?

- What proportion of faculty members have a terminal degree, such as a Ph.D., law degree, master of fine arts, or master of business administration? While a degree is no guarantee of knowledge or the ability to convey knowledge, it's a sign that they've gone through extensive learning themselves.

- Do most faculty have actual experience in their fields? If their biographies or résumés are in the catalog or on the Web, check a few in your planned major. Do they list jobs, consultancies, or research for businesses, government entities, or nonprofit organizations? Or have they spent their entire life as adults on campuses as students and faculty members?

- Do full-time and part-time faculty hold regularly scheduled office hours, and are they available by appointment as well?

- Will you be assigned to a professor in your major as your academic advisor or mentor, and do you have a choice in that assignment? Sarah

Lawrence College (New York) uses a system called "donning" in which each student designs his or her own program with an assigned faculty advisor, who will be available for continuing guidance. The system is similar to that of Oxford and Cambridge, two British universities that use dons. "Don and donee work together to plan a course of study that best suits the academic needs, aspirations, and career goals of the student," the college says.

- Do faculty members work with student organizations in the field, such as campus chapters of professional and career-focused associations?
- What is the male-female ratio among the faculty, both campuswide and in your prospective major?
- Does the college give awards for outstanding teaching? If so, who gets them?
- How diverse is the faculty in terms of race, ethnicity, religion, and nationality?
- How large will your classes be? If you're transferring from a large school, you may already have sat through introductory lectures for three hundred students in economics, sociology, history, or psychology. The nature of some majors requires mostly small classes, such as laboratory-oriented sciences, journalism, dance, or audiology.
- Will professors in your departments help design independent study opportunities or research projects that interest you?

RETENTION

What proportion of students at your target school complete their degrees and, on average, how long does it take them? That's what retention is all about. There are lots of reasons why students leave, among them money, personal crises, inadequate academic challenge, lack of direction and self-control, homesickness, poor study skills, and an inappropriate mesh between them and their school. "Retention is the lifeblood of an institution. It says a lot about the quality of the experience for the student. It's something a university has to be responsive to," Johnetta Cross Brazzell, the vice president for student affairs at the University of Arkansas in Fayetteville told *Black Issues in Higher Education* magazine.

With your added maturity as a transfer student, the chances of completing the program should be higher than for freshmen. At the University of Washington, for instance, about 80 percent of transfer students graduate, in contrast to a 70-percent rate for those who arrive as freshmen.

Dropout rates are rising at some schools, costing them lost tuition, fees, and federal or state aid. Fortunately, some are responding with enhanced learning and guidance opportunities, enrichment activities, more personal contact, and financial incentives. Even so, the disappointing truth is that some colleges bemoan high attrition rates but don't do enough to retain students and ensure their success. A proven commitment to keep students through graduation should resonate among potential transfers.

That's why you need to look at the school's retention rate as part of your assessment process.

MENU OF MAJORS

One of the principal reasons students transfer is the array of majors at the target schools they consider. While most colleges offer the standard range of majors in social sciences, natural sciences, and humanities, there are well over a

"A revolution appears to be sweeping the campuses of the nation's colleges and universities, and it is based on a simple credo: The success of an institution and the success of its students are inseparable.

Retention is . . . the best indicator that an institution is meeting its goal of student satisfaction and success. It is a measure of how much student growth and learning takes place, how valued and respected students feel on campus, and how effectively the campus delivers what students expect, need, and want. When these conditions are met, students find a way to stay in school, despite external and personal pressures."

—Randi S. Levitz, Lee Noel, and Beth J. Richter in "Strategic Moves for Retention Success" in *New Directions for Higher Education* hundred majors available at four-year colleges, and lots more at community and junior colleges.

Because you've already taken college-level courses in several disciplines, you probably now have a firmer idea of what you want to concentrate on than you did in your first semester. Chemistry, biology, or German may have seized your imagination and piqued your curiosity in high school, but a college class or two in the field may have quickly squelched that interest. On the other hand, a required art history course or accounting elective at your current college may have jump-started an unfamiliar but exciting intellectual or career interest that you can best pursue at a different college.

As you examine potential schools, look beyond the glitzy catalogs, videos, and high-tech labs to the menu of majors offered there. Read through the catalog—in print or online—to scope out the departments of interest and, equally important, the course descriptions. Be sure to check how often the listed specialized or advanced courses are offered. Some may be held only in alternative years, or even less frequently, but remain in the catalog as padding, making it appear the department's offerings are more extensive than reality shows.

If you have a major (or more than one) in mind, ask these questions:

- What's the apparent focus of the department, based on its philosophy and the courses in the catalog? In English, it could be literature, creative writing, technical writing, mass media, high school teaching of English, or a combination.

- How does the selection of courses compare to what you've already taken or have available at your current college? If there are only a handful of topics you haven't covered so far, you may find yourself bored or frustrated at the new college.

- How large is the faculty in that department? The more instructors, the more variety in teaching styles and intellectual interests. Also, the more instructors, the greater the likelihood that new or experimental classes will be added.

- Who teaches undergraduates? Full-time faculty? Part-time adjuncts? Graduate assistants? A mix?

- How popular is the major? Is there a cap on the number of students admitted to the major? If so, how are they selected (grade point average, first-come-first-served, class ranking, lottery, competitive application) and are you at an advantage or disadvantage as a transfer student? Is it harder to get into individual courses if the major is crowded?

- What's the department's reputation? This is an especially significant factor when you look for a job in the field, seek an internship, or apply to graduate school. A highly regarded college may have some majors that rank only average in national surveys and evaluations. The opposite is true as well, because some stellar departments prosper at lesser-known or lesser-regarded schools.

- What requirements does the department impose, beyond the college's broader requirements? Check on prerequisites, the number of credits you need in that major, whether an internship or work experience is necessary, whether there's a foreign language requirement, and the job and career prospects for majors after graduation.

Also, look at related fields. Say you've got your heart set on moving to a particular college. If the major you have in mind isn't available there and if there are still compelling reasons to go there, investigate allied areas of study. There may be no fisheries major but you may find enough fisheries courses to satisfy you under biological sciences or zoology. No theater department? Are there enough relevant courses under English, dance, and music? A college without a journalism department may offer journalism classes under English, communications, or media studies.

You may also want—or need—a minor or a cognate. If so, make sure the college has at least one that grabs you. (A minor is a concentration of related courses, but fewer than necessary for a major. A cognate is a field of study related to your major but offered by a different department or group of departments.) For example, an economics major may minor in political science or international relations, or choose a cognate in finance or marketing.

A few colleges *don't* have traditional majors—or majors at all—and, instead, stand on a platform of holistic and integrated learning. This may be an ideal match for your intellectual orientation and self-discipline, or you may feel out of place without the familiar, formal structures of most U.S. and Canadian colleges.

For example, Hampshire College (Massachusetts) has replaced its single-subject departments with five interdisciplinary schools: Humanities, Arts, and Cultural Studies; Interdisciplinary Arts; Natural Science; Cognitive Science; and Social Science. "This flexible structure," the college says, "permits a great richness and variety of academic activity." St. John's College (New Mexico and Maryland) goes further and follows a curriculum based on the Great Books, without any majors. It says, "Through the reading of original texts, students reflect on the great expressions of the Western tradition from ancient Greece to modern times. Students study from the classics of literature, philosophy, theology, psychology, political science, economics, history, mathematics, laboratory sciences, music, and the visual arts." Despite the absence of formal majors, the college says its students suffer no disadvantage in applying for graduate or professional school.

INTERDISCIPLINARY AND MULTIDISCIPLINARY STUDIES

In the workplace, rigid barriers that once separated careers and professions are crumbling. Engineers today are expected to understand budgets, nurses confront questions of medical ethics, psychologists counsel patients on problems with faith and spirituality, farmers use global positioning satellites to plant their crops, and teachers deal with sociological problems. Although this isn't the way most high schools teach—remember those separate periods for math, biology, and civics, for example?—a multidisciplinary approach makes sense when you think about it.

Many colleges are putting more emphasis on multidisciplinary studies. That doesn't mean they've said good-bye to traditional, discrete majors such as English, political science, or botany. Instead, it means students will learn about—and, increasingly, major in—interrelated fields that reflect how the working world operates, whether in the private sector such as manufacturing, in nonprofit organizations, or in government.

Perhaps the longest established and best-known multidisciplinary fields are ethnic studies programs such as African-American, Asian-American, Jewish, Native American, or Latino studies. Those majors put together a diverse but inter-linked curriculum of courses in history, literature, music, religion, foreign language, sociology, and other traditional fields.

Regional and geographic specializations are also well established in some colleges. If you major in Southeast Asian studies, for instance, your courses could span history, languages, geography, art, religion, architecture, philosophy, and music. If urban studies is your choice, there'll be history, political science, geography, architecture, anthropology, economics, criminal justice, health, and public administration.

Period studies fill another niche. Whether your focus is the Middle Ages or the twentieth century, your menu can include history, languages, art, media studies, music, literature, sociology, and philosophy.

Environmental studies is another burgeoning multidisciplinary field. Students may immerse themselves in a combination of traditional science courses such as biology and zoology, traditional applied sciences courses such as forestry and horticulture, traditional business courses such as public administration and accounting, traditional social science courses such as economics and political science, and perhaps a couple of selections from engineering, parks and recreation, or communications.

Here are some of the other types of multidisciplinary majors you'll find across the country, with related fields:

• International relations: history; political science; geography; economics; languages; business

"There are many fields of study that are unfamiliar to you. But what's new and strange could prove to be ideal for you—if you find it."

—Eric Freedman and Edward Hoffman in *What to Study: 101 Fields in a Flash*
(Kaplan and Simon & Schuster, latest editon)

- Resource development: sociology; geography; economics; law; forestry; agriculture; parks and recreation; anthropology; fisheries and wildlife
- Gender studies: psychology; sociology; history; literature; health; art; music; anthropology; political science
- War and peace studies: history; political science; languages; anthropology; economics; sociology; engineering

Also, when you explore transfer opportunities, ask whether the college will let you piece together an individualized, thematic major if the one you want isn't formally available. One advantage to this flexibility is the ability to tailor a curriculum that most closely coincides with your interests. Another advantage is the chance to get to know faculty members in a variety of disciplines and who have open minds toward experimentation in higher education and the learning process.

ACADEMIC OPTIONS

A key part of scoping out a college is probing out-of-classroom academic opportunities. As you already recognize, much learning takes place beyond the borders of traditional classes.

Here are more than a dozen arenas where nontraditional, innovative, or flexible learning can occur, enriching the academic experience, accommodating your personal and intellectual needs, and making you a better-prepared contender for jobs or graduate and professional programs:

OVERSEAS STUDY

At a few colleges, virtually all undergrads spend a semester or a year abroad. Many other schools actively encourage such opportunities, either by running their own overseas programs or by partnering with host institutions in other countries. See how well those destinations tie in to your major or minor.

If your target school has such options, be sure to ask about the costs of overseas study, availability of financial aid, and transferability and applicability of credits. Increasingly, colleges are trying to keep the cost of overseas study about the same as if you stayed on campus for the same semester or academic year.

INTERNSHIPS

If I were an employer, the successful performance of at least one internship—whether paid, for credit, or volunteer—would move a job applicant way up on my list of potential hires. Although some majors such as teacher education, nursing, and physical therapy require an internship to graduate, any student in any major can gain experience, connections, and recommendations from one.

A school's location may affect the availability of internships, especially part-time internships during the academic year. Typically, a college in a metropolitan area will have more potential placements to draw from than one in a small, isolated community. Yet there are opportunities, even outside big cities. Champlain College (Vermont) boasts that 96 percent of students in its two-year and four-year degree programs do internships.

Ask whether the college or your department helps line up internships, whether they are available for credit or for pay, and how your course schedule can accommodate an internship.

CO-OP PROGRAMS

Some colleges pride themselves on aggressive cooperative education programs in which students alternate paid, major-related jobs with courses on campus. According to Wilberforce University (Ohio), which requires all its students to participate in a co-op program, "Cooperative education gives the students the advantage of testing these interests early on in their undergraduate program. The combination of academic study and cooperative education work experience produces an overall learning experience that gives the student greater meaning of their academic program and direction to their career development."

Those programs generally take longer to complete than attending classes full time, but they can dramatically ease the financial burden of attending school and can provide a pipeline to a permanent position after you graduate. You, the college, and the employer will sign some type of training agreement that lays out each party's responsibilities and the learning objectives. Expect to submit a final report and undergo evaluation by both your work supervisor and your faculty coordinator.

BENEFITS OF COOPERATIVE EDUCATION

- Helps in career decision-making. You can reality-test careers and make choices based on on-the-job experience in a chosen field. As a result of cooperative education, you have a clearer and more specific sense of your career objectives than do students in traditional college programs.
- Allows you to test classroom learning in the laboratory of the real world.
- Enables you to pay for a significant portion of your college expenses through earnings from your cooperative education work experience.
- Provides a means of financial assistance that is available to all students, regardless of their family income levels or other financial aid arrangements. The opportunity to earn income while pursuing a college degree is often an added incentive for many first-generation college students.
- Improves post-graduation employment prospects by giving you valuable work experience.
- Teaches you valuable job search skills such as résumé writing, interviewing techniques, and company research.
- Provides you with a more direct relationship between your college major and full-time permanent employment, as well as a more direct relationship between your current employment and career plans.
- Helps you in the development of an understanding of human relationships and social skills required to work more effectively with others as members of a team.
- Provides you an opportunity to observe the social skills and attitudes held by other professionals in one's field, and learn about different corporate cultures.
- Increases your marketability after graduation to receive a higher starting salary and accelerate your upward mobility.

—Wilberforce University (Ohio)

Your questions should include the impact of participation on your academic progress, the relevance of co-op placements to your major and career goals, and the effect of your salary on financial aid eligibility. If you're an international student, be sure your visa or citizenship status will allow you hold a paid co-op job. Waterloo University (Ontario) requires Canadian citizenship or permanent residence status to participate in its co-op program.

In the United States, international students need authorization to legally work in any cooperative job, according to Northeastern University (Massachusetts), which says, "International students are subject to U.S. immigration regulations that govern their eligibility for employment." A university office should be designated to sign documents that permit legal employment, and eligible students should get authorization before starting their first day of co-op work. The university adds, "International students on F-1 and J-1 visas working in cooperative education positions are subject to the withholding of federal, state, and local income taxes unless they are exempt by provision of a tax treaty. Students on F-1 and J-1 visas are generally exempt from Social Security and Medicare taxes while working in co-op positions."

SERVICE LEARNING

Do your target colleges encourage community service and volunteer work and, if so, how aggressively? Volunteering is an excellent way to gain experience, find references, and test the waters in a field that interests you. It also helps you learn to better balance your time and energy.

Check whether a target school has a center or office that coordinates community service, matching students to nonprofit agencies and organizations that need their skills. Ask for the names of recent volunteers willing to discuss their experiences, pro and con.

INDEPENDENT STUDY

The beauty of independent study is the chance to craft a course when the existing catalog doesn't provide exactly what you want or if you're dissatisfied with the depth or pace of a standard offering. For instance, a history major deeply interested in the Vietnam War era in the United States or in Canada's nonviolent move to independence from Great Britain may design a curriculum of readings and research to explore those topics if they're omitted or touched on only lightly in the standard U.S. or Canadian history curriculum. An English or theater major might do the same thing to examine in detail the life and works of a favorite playwright.

Be sure to get answers to these questions: Are faculty members open to assisting one-on-one as you craft and carry out an independent study? How much time and work are expected on your part in comparison to standard courses? How will the credits and grades be calculated?

One place to look for independent study opportunities is through specialized or thematic research programs and centers on campus. The University of Wisconsin at Milwaukee alone lists more than sixty, ranging from centers on nursing history, early childhood education, and small business development for centers for Great Lakes studies, alternative fuels, and Canadian-American policy issues.

SELF-PACED STUDY

Self-paced courses follow the same content, textbooks, assignments, and objectives as traditional classroom classes. There may be a mandatory orientation session, but after that, you do the work at your own speed. This option may prove most useful if you want or need two courses that meet at the same time, if you travel a lot and would miss too many sessions, or if a course doesn't fit your job schedule. Exams may be given on campus.

JOINT BACHELOR'S–MASTER'S PROGRAMS

If you've got graduate or professional school in mind, consider universities that offer combined bachelor's and master's programs. If you do well as an undergraduate, you're assured admission to the university's professional or graduate school and you can shave time off the advanced program by coordinating courses and, perhaps, attending summer session. A typical model lets you earn a bachelor's degree and an MBA in five years rather than six.

HONORS PROGRAMS

Is there an active program for students with superior grade point averages? This type of program goes beyond a simple dean's list based on high grades and can include selected seminars, special guest speakers, and honors-designated sections of courses. At some colleges, students in the honors program are eligible for additional scholarships and grants.

CONSORTIA

Increasingly, colleges belong to consortia that allow their students to take courses at other schools and earn full credit toward their degrees. That means you can transfer to a small school where you feel most comfortable but take classes at a nearby larger institution that offers more classes of interest to you. Or say you transfer to a technology-oriented or engineering-oriented school and want to take a couple of music electives to hone your euphonium or oboe skills: You can do that at a consortium partner that offers a strong performing arts program.

Find out whether there's a tuition differential if the other school is more or less expensive than your own. Check transportation between the campuses, academic calendars—they may have different vacation weeks—and grading systems.

Not all consortia are local. As an example, thirteen Christian liberal arts colleges belong to the Christian College Consortium. They're scattered across more than a half-dozen states including Indiana, Kentucky, Oregon, Illinois, Ohio, Pennsylvania, and Massachusetts. Under this type of arrangement, students can spend a semester at another consortium campus and take part in cooperative off-campus and international programs.

ONLINE COURSES

The Internet is expanding the "delivery" of teaching and education. One way that's happening is through online or "virtual" courses that you can take anywhere and anytime. They may enable you to progress smoothly toward your degree after transferring if work or family commitments limit the times you can physically be on campus. Another strength is that a specialized or advanced online course can be offered even when there would be insufficient enrollment to justify it economically as a traditional course. And some colleges now offer fully accredited online degree programs.

Florida International University groups its 350-plus online courses into three formats: Web-assisted, in which all classes meet in a classroom and use the Web as a supplemental tool; campus/online, in which half the course is taught online and the other half in a classroom; and fully online, in which the entire course takes place over the Internet, except for orientation and proctored testing.

In some instances, the content and structure closely parallel that of traditional courses. In others, course content is designed specifically to take advantage of the medium's exciting interactive potential, making maximum use of linking, chat sessions, and an electronic library of readings. Either way, the syllabus and assignments are accessible from the Web, and papers and projects generally can be "handed in" electronically as well. Exams can be completed online or on campus, depending on the instructor's wishes.

WEEKEND COURSES AND PROGRAMS

It's often hard to squeeze in a full course load with the demands of a job and family obligations. One alternative is taking weekend classes. They require the same number of contact—classroom or lab—hours as traditional classes, and may run in blocks such as three weeks, six weeks, or nine weeks. There are several ways a college may structure them. The most common are all-day Saturdays, all-day Sundays, a combination of Saturdays and Sundays, or Friday evenings and all-day Saturdays. Weekends may not run consecutively.

Content and the amount of work expected will be similar to that for traditional classes, but the format and presentation are apt to vary.

Two other advantages: Parking on campus will be easier on the weekend, and you'll probably get to know your classmates better from 9 A.M.-to-4 P.M. exposure than from a typical hour-long session twice a week.

FIELD RESEARCH SITES

For most new high school graduates, research goals aren't even a blip on the radar screen. Now that you've been in college for a while, however, you may already have had experience doing research outside the lab, the library, or the classroom for at least one course. In many areas of study, field research is both essential and exciting.

The list of majors that involve field research is lengthy indeed, from botany, oceanography, fisheries, and agronomy to environmental sciences, forestry, anthropology, and animal science. Find out whether the colleges you're considering have off-campus facilities like research farms and forests, and fish hatcheries. Every state has at least one land grant college, and that may mean agricultural experiment stations and county services involving home economics, agriculture, forestry, fire service, child development, nutrition, and economic development.

SATELLITE SITES

If you plan to live far from the college and commute, inquire whether any classes are offered off campus at satellite sites. This pattern is most common among community colleges that offer courses at high schools within their districts. However, many major universities have off-campus centers as well, such as those located in suburban and urban areas. Often, regular faculty teach these classes, although adjuncts may teach others.

Please note that in the drive to recruit, retain, and motivate students, a number of colleges allow variations or combinations of these types of enrichment options. One such approach allows students to design their own majors. Another is the so-called "open" curriculum to enable students to develop their own programs. Participation may be limited to students who demonstrate above-average maturity and special talents or interests. Such flexible, innovative opportunities often are organized around a multidisciplinary theme and could include a mixture of traditional and online courses, independent study, overseas study, and classwork at other consortium campuses, plus the courses you've taken at your current and previous school. In all these situations, expect to work closely with one or more faculty advisors.

GRADUATION REQUIREMENTS

What will you need to get out with a bachelor's degree? Graduation requirements vary from college to college, and you should find out the answers ahead of time because the answers may affect your decision where to transfer. In many cases, you'll need a minimum number of semesters—usually four—at your new school, although you may be able to count a semester or year abroad in a program run or approved by that college.

Here are some questions you should ask before you transfer:

- Do you need a minimum number of semesters of a foreign language or will you have to pass a proficiency test? If you need to achieve proficiency in a foreign language, can you meet that requirement in a language that's not offered by your new college?
- Is there a minimum number of mandatory courses in math, literature, writing, religious studies, or another field outside your major or minor? Are there fine arts or humanities requirements, a rhetoric or speech requirement, compulsory physical education, or a computer proficiency standard? A study by the Association of American Colleges and Universities found that more than half of U.S. colleges surveyed require students to take diversity courses, although they vary tremendously on what will meet that requirement. (Chapter 10, "Solve the Mysteries of Transferring Credits," discusses the evaluation of transfer credits and how to determine whether your previous coursework will fulfill any of these requirements.)
- How many credits overall will you need for an associate's or bachelor's degree at the target college? What core, distribution, or general education requirements must all students meet? What's the minimum GPA to graduate, both in your major and overall? What's the maximum number of credits you can take at another institution?

Don't be seduced by glamour. Ultimately, academics should be your principal motivator because without that, a degree is merely an expensive but empty piece of paper, no matter how renowned your school is. We all learn in a variety of ways, so your ideal colleges are those that offer avenues of learning that fit your aptitudes and interests. That's why you must ask the right questions to determine what avenues of learning are available.

MAKE THE
CAMPUS
VISIT

and out-of-date? Does the bustle of an elevated train passing a lecture hall feel vibrant—or disconcerting? Although you can't always judge a book by its cover, you *can* judge a college in part by how its academic and social environments feel to you. There's no substitute for a visit because videos, brochures, and off-campus interviews can't provide as complete a picture of a campus. And if you eventually attend a school you've visited, you'll be familiar with the campus lay-out when you arrive for classes months later.

The fit of the college matters a great deal. How comfortable is the environment? How friendly are the people?

Timothy MacGregor, who transferred from a school in Massachusetts to Wesleyan University (Connecticut), says the main benefits of his visits to three target campuses were getting a sense of student life, seeing the living arrangements, and deciding whether or not he'd fit in well.

A student who transferred to Green Mountain College (Vermont) says the three main benefits from her visit were an opportunity to get a feel for the college's culture, to see its academic mission in action, and to help decide whether she and the school were compatible.

As a prospective transfer student, you have an advantage over high school students searching for their first college. That's because you have a reference point, namely the campus and community of your current school. It's only natural to make comparisons, positive and negative, between the places you're familiar with and any place you may spend the next few years. You'll make more realistic

"Taking an afternoon to visit with advisors in admissions, academic advising, and financial aid can be time well spent, and it may eliminate misunderstandings and frustration during the actual transfer process."

—Samuel Collie, director of student financial aid, Portland State University (Oregon)

assessments that way. Visits also let you compare and contrast potential schools among themselves.

Here are suggestions for how to profit the most from a college visit—whether it's across the country, across the state, or merely across town.

PLAN AHEAD

Before you set out, think over your schedule and any necessary preparation. A weekday when school's in session is the best time to see a campus as it really is, even if it means missing classes or rearranging your work schedule. If possible, avoid holidays, weekends, and semester breaks. These times may be more convenient for you, but it's harder to get an interview, take a tour, attend classes, talk with students, or spend a night on campus.

Once you pinpoint a date to visit, sign up to stay in a dorm, housing co-op, fraternity, sorority, or on-campus apartment if the school has them. Even if you don't intend to live on campus after you transfer, this will give you a better feel for how other students live—and a chance to talk candidly with them in a casual setting. Many admissions offices will line up a host, who may be matched according to your potential major, hometown, or other interests. You may need to give a specified amount of advance notice so arrangements can be made.

If the college doesn't make such arrangements, you may be able to stay overnight with somebody who went to your high school or who transferred from your present college. Ask your former high school guidance counselor or your community college transfer advisor for the names of contacts.

Make long trips efficient by planning stops along the route. If you drive from New England to a North Carolina college, schedule visits at other schools along the way, perhaps in the New York City, Washington, or Baltimore areas. That will give you more reference points to make comparisons when you arrive at your primary destinations. In addition, it raises the possibility of a pleasant surprise from a college that hadn't been high on your initial list.

Get psyched. Mental preparation is vital too. Read the recruitment material and guidebooks ahead of time. They should give you an idea of how many students attend that college and what type of setting—city, rural, small town, or suburban—it's in. Check if the college literature answers these questions:

- What academic programs and extracurricular activities are available?
- What facilities and amenities matter most to you?
- How can the college help you overcome financial obstacles?
- If you have a disability, how accessible are the buildings?

With that type of list of questions in hand, you can seek answers at the best possible place—on campus.

When you know your anticipated travel dates, phone the admissions office as soon as possible to arrange the visit. For example, you may want to book an interview with admissions and financial aid officers who specialize in transfer students, even if such interviews aren't required. Ask whether you should bring copies of your transcript, portfolio, or other documents.

You may also want to set up an interview with faculty members in the major you're interested in or with a coach. Also ask the admissions office to suggest classes in your fields of interest that you can sit in on.

Use the admissions staff as a resource. They're the college's front line of interpreters to prospective students—customers, if you want to think of yourself that way—and well-informed sources for referrals and practical advice. In some schools, the admissions office will set appointments with the faculty.

TOUR THE CAMPUS

Don't zip in and out of the admissions office and then head home. Take a tour to get a more formal overview of the campus and a student's perspective of the

"Students who come for a campus informational visit or those who request an interview are seeking an opportunity to understand the uniqueness of the campus and to share their own special qualities."

—Joyce E. Smith in "Recruitment: Student Outreach Strategies" in *Handbook for the College Admissions Process* (Greenwood Press, latest edition)

CAMPUS VISIT CHECKLIST

IN ADVANCE

- Get transcripts, recommendations, or other records you might need or want to have handy.
- Make appointments and confirm the precise location of each one.
- Decide if you want a parent, friend, or somebody else to accompany you.
- Prepare questions. What do you want to know by the time your visit is over?
- Check on classes you might want to sit in on, and get their exact times and locations. Ask the admissions office to notify the professor in advance that you'd like to attend.
- Get directions to campus and to your first stop there. See if there's a campus map on the Web site, or ask the admissions office to mail you one. Mark all your expected stops with a highlighter.
- Find out about visitor parking. If you're traveling by train, bus, or plane, ask about the most convenient and reasonable ways to reach campus from the terminal, station, or airport.
- Get in touch with any friends or friends-of-friends already at the school. See if you can get together during your visit.
- For overnight visits, arrange for an on-campus stay or reserve a room at a nearby motel. Some motels have special discounts for college-affiliated visitors.
- Pack appropriate clothes. Interviews are professional meetings, so you want to make a positive impression with admissions, financial aid, academic, and athletic staff.
- Whether or not you drive there, give yourself a comfortable time cushion so you don't feel rushed. It's better to arrive early and wait for your first appointment or tour than to arrive late, be embarrassed, and feel even more pressure.

ON ARRIVAL AT CAMPUS

- Double-check the map to orient yourself.
- Stress is natural. Give yourself a few minutes to relax, stretch, and breathe deeply before you walk into your first appointment, meeting, or class.
- Pick up a campus paper and look at bulletin boards as you walk around for announcements of events going on that day or evening.
- Take brochures, catalogs, and flyers that might prove useful in the application process or in the selection of courses, majors, and extracurricular activities.
- You might want to take a camera and shoot a few photos.
- Jot quick notes on the experience and your impressions. Write down any new questions that occur to you.

AFTER YOU GET HOME

- Write a short thank-you note or e-mail to each person you meet—admissions counselor, financial aid advisor, faculty, coach, music director, tour guide, and others. Don't forget your dorm host. It's courteous and, if you transfer there, they are more likely to remember you and help you.
- Review the written material you picked up and any notes you took. Put down your reactions, favorable and unfavorable, as a reminder when it comes time to decide whether or not to transfer there.
- Follow up on any unanswered questions, whether they were on the original list that you prepared in advance or whether they occurred to you during the visit. Write, call, or e-mail to find the answers.
- A productive campus visit is more than a sightseeing event. It's your opportunity to get a tangible feel for a campus, to envision yourself walking down its paths and through its corridors, and to give real-world depth to the words and photos in a catalog, brochure, Web site, or video. In other words, being there is the best way to see if you can envision yourself there.

school, even if you've visited before to see a friend or to attend a football game or concert.

The guides are generally enthusiastic undergrads with a wealth of information and inside tips you may not find in the official recruitment brochures. They can offer a combination of personal experiences and anecdotes about students, professors, and campus personalities and culture. You're also likely to get frank answers to tough questions about such topics as campus safety, discrimination, grading policies, adequacy of facilities, and attitudes toward studying and partying.

Some colleges offer specialized tours that cover the libraries, sports facilities, research labs, performing arts centers, or horticultural gardens. Ask whether such a specific tour is scheduled or can be arranged.

CHECK OUT CLASSES

As you know by now, college teaching styles differ not only from high school but also from professor to professor. The admissions office can prepare a schedule of appropriate classes, ranging from large introductory lectures to small, advanced seminars. Let the admissions staff know what majors most interest you and if there are particular faculty members you'd most like to see in action.

Do some of that homework yourself. Use the printed catalog or online version to examine course descriptions for ones that pique your curiosity. If the semester schedule is on the Web, see which of those classes will be held while you're on campus.

A single class or two is no guarantee of how other courses and instructors operate, but a few hours spent in one or two classrooms, labs, or lecture halls will provide a taste of what the academic atmosphere is like at each school you visit. Feel free, before or after the class, to introduce yourself to the professor as a prospective transfer student and ask about the course and the department.

EXPLORE THE FACILITIES

Dorms and dining halls should be at the top of your check-it-out list of must-see facilities if you intend to live on campus, even if it's just for your first semester

CLASS VISIT REPORT CARD

Since you're already a college student, you have a firm basis for comparison when you sit in on a class. Try to answer these questions:

• Are students attentive and engaged? Do they take notes and follow what the professor is saying? Or are they talking among themselves, reading newspapers, and constantly checking the clock?

• Do students seem prepared? Can you tell whether most of them have done their assigned reading or homework?

• Is mutual respect apparent between the professor and students? Does the professor disparage or talk down to the class? Do students drift in late and slink out early?

• Is there give and take? Do students seem comfortable asking questions or even disagreeing with the professor? If the professor's style is to call on students randomly, do they appear at ease with that format, or resentful? Does the professor hang around after class formally ends to address students' individual concerns?

• Even if the class is more advanced than what you're used to, can you follow the gist of the lecture, experiment, or presentation?

• Is the facility conducive for learning? Can you see and hear well enough? Does the equipment—overhead projectors, audiovisual gear, laboratory instruments, and computers—work properly?

after transferring. For some students, dorm arrangements, costs, and policies are decisive factors in choosing among similar schools. If you can't stay the night, at least ask to look in a typical room or suite. And talk to students who live there.

Remember that dorms can vary tremendously, even on the same campus. Look carefully:

- Are the buildings run-down or in good condition?
- Are rooms comfortable or overcrowded?
- Are there lounges for studying and socializing?
- Is there a computer lab in the building or close by?
- What are the policies for assigning roommates and suitemates?
- Are there co-ed, nonsmoking, or alcohol-free and drug-free dorms?
- Are there Internet connections for computers in the rooms?

Find out about theme-based housing such as international studies, foreign languages, athletics, ethnic studies, or environmental activism. You also may want to tour fraternity or sorority housing if you're considering becoming part of the Greek system.

If you're interested in intercollegiate teams, intramurals, or simply staying in shape, explore the athletic facilities. Are there convenient open hours for swimming, ice skating, racquetball, and tennis, or are they virtually always reserved for teams and physical education classes?

If drama is your passion, walk around the theater and backstage, and find out about opportunities to take part in student productions. If it's music, look at the auditorium and other facilities, and check into practice rooms, private lessons, and band, orchestra, or choir programs.

For more insights into campus life during your visit, read the campus newspaper and bulletin boards for announcements of lectures, plays, movies, concerts, and religious services.

By all means, take advantage of what's going on while you're touring the school. It might be a tuba concert, a guest speaker, an art exhibit, a basketball game, a rodeo, a religious service, an orchestra rehearsal, a fund-raising 5K walk, an international holiday fair, or a chess club meeting.

Keep alert for the mood and cultural mix on campus—the good, the bad, and the ugly. The good may be students playing Frisbee or studying on the quad and a bustling student union. The bad may be long cafeteria lines, broken computers in the labs, or sharply limited library hours. The ugly may be overflowing trash barrels, littered pathways, and dirty corridors.

DO THE TOWN

Again, you can't simply rely on the catalog and Web site for an accurate description of the surrounding community. Drive or walk around the college's neighborhood. See what stores and facilities are convenient. Other things to check out are:

- How well lit are the streets at night?
- What's the apparent condition of off-campus housing?
- Is parking available at the apartment complexes, fraternity and sorority houses, or other accommodations where you might live?
- How reliable is the area's public transit system, and when does it operate?
- If you intend to live off campus and don't have a car, how will you get home late at night after the library closes if the buses stop running at 9 P.M.?

WHEN YOU'RE DONE

Of course, first impressions aren't always accurate, but you probably won't leave feeling ambivalent or so-so about the college after a visit. Often, you'll be able to say whether or not you'd feel comfortable there. And if you have any uncertainties when it comes time to make a decision, consider a second visit.

Remember that a campus visit is like watching five minutes of a two-hour movie. It's only a sampling of a complex world. Even so, it's a valuable tool for assessing a college and how well it fits you.

FACILITIES CHECKLIST

Some campuses have only a handful of buildings, while others boast more than one hundred. Regardless of size, check these out:

LIBRARIES

- Hours
- Computerized catalog and research databases
- Availability of professional reference librarians
- Depth of collection
- Specialized collections
- Photocopiers
- Study space
- Availability of interlibrary loans

DORMS

- Condition and maintenance
- Spaciousness
- Noise levels
- Internet hook-ups
- Computer facilities
- Proximity to classes
- Recreational facilities
- Parking
- Supervisory and advising staff

CLASSROOMS AND LABORATORIES

- Up-to-date audiovisual, computer, and scientific equipment
- Cleanliness
- Comfortable desks or seats

RECREATION AND ATHLETIC FACILITIES

- Condition
- Hours
- Equipment
- Experienced coaching and training staff
- Recreational and intramural access

ANCILLARY BUILDINGS

- Museums
- Theater and concert halls
- Art galleries
- Student union
- Religious facilities
- Health clinic

PLACEMENT AND ADVISING OFFICES

- Experienced counseling and financial aid staff
- Easy access to information about jobs, internships, and graduate studies

7

COMMUNITY COLLEGE

TRANSFER SERVICES

ONE MEASURE OF SUCCESS FOR COMMUNITY AND

junior colleges is the proportion of their graduates who go on to four-year schools after earning an associate's degree or certificate. That's one reason why they offer an array of services to help their students successfully navigate the transfer application and transition processes.

Typically, those services include running a transfer services office, hosting college fairs that draw representatives from dozens of four-year colleges, coordinating the visits of recruiters, holding individual and group counseling sessions, providing transcripts and recommendations, and critiquing applications and essays. They arrange transfer workshops and write how-to-transfer articles for the campus newspaper.

Some prepare directories with information about the requirements of the four-year institutions that their students most often go to. These directories may list minimum GPA and test requirements, maximum number of transferable credits, application deadlines and fees, and the address, phone, and e-mail of the admissions office or transfer specialist.

PLANNING FOR YOUR TRANSFER

Community and junior college advisors stress the importance of identifying target schools early on and of planning your transfer from the start, especially if you already have a specific career or professional goal in mind. As Charlotte Reall, senior admissions officer at Community College of Rhode Island, puts it, "The transfer process begins during the first semester." One principal reason is to help map out your course selection during your time there. Along such lines, the Collin County Community College District (Texas) gives would-be teachers a handout listing the state requirements for teacher education, including the number of credits required in such areas as speech, American history, math, and fine arts.

In its guidelines for prospective transfer students, Rose-Hulman Institute of Technology (Indiana) encourages would-be applicants "to enroll in calculus,

As the University of California at Los Angeles tells its prospective transfer students, "Meeting requirements in advance will give you more freedom when selecting courses once you enroll in the university. You may also be able to complete your undergraduate education within four years, without having to attend additional terms to meet requirements or take prerequisites."

chemistry, and calculus-based physics" at their present institutions, adding: "These courses are freshman requirements for most majors at Rose-Hulman. Other courses that we suggest for transfer students, but do not require, are computer programming, computer graphics, and/or humanities and social sciences courses."

Your two-year college may provide several distinct tracks toward an associate's degree, with some aimed at anticipated transfers and others intended to be terminal. The distinction is that not all courses in a career-oriented track may transfer smoothly if you later decide to switch schools and earn a bachelor's degree.

Here's an example of such a system from Red Rocks Community College (Colorado), which has three transfer-oriented tracks and two terminal-oriented tracks:

- Associate of Arts, "university parallel," for students who intend to transfer and want a liberal arts emphasis, such as art, business, economics, English, languages, history, humanities, political science, psychology, sociology, communication, or theater
- Associate of Science, "university parallel," for students with a science-related emphasis in such areas as biology, biotechnology, chemistry, computer science, pre-engineering, geology, math, prenursing, or physics
- Associate of General Studies-Specialist, "articulated transfer," for students who want to meet the core general education transfer requirements with a career-oriented emphasis such as criminal justice, early childhood education, or multimedia technology

For students who pursue the two terminal-oriented tracks—Associate of General Studies-Generalist and Associate of Applied Science—four-year colleges will consider courses for transfer on an individual basis.

Select classes carefully. The catalog may identify those courses that are unlikely to transfer. As an example, Red Rocks has two types of language courses. The catalog description of the "conversational Spanish" sequence notes, "This course may not transfer to a four-year institution," while the "foreign language" sequence will.

Take advantage of partnerships between your two-year college and any four-year schools you'd like to transfer to. For example, Southern Illinois University runs what it calls an "individualized two plus two" program for students who have a firm goal in mind when they start community college and who intend to transfer after earning an associate's degree. Participants receive an exact list of courses required to complete a bachelor's degree and a list of courses at their community college that will transfer directly to their chosen major. The program evaluates each student's community college work each semester, keeps community college advisors informed of the students' plans, and provides "constant feed-back" while the students are still at their community college. Participants who are considering a change in future majors can use the Southern Illinois Web site to examine the potential academic impact of such a change.

COUNSELING AND SUPPORT SERVICES

Another essential aspect of community college services is helping their students evaluate transfer credits. One place to start is with the formal articulation agreements between your community college and some four-year institutions. These include course-by-course equivalencies negotiated by the participating schools. For more information on the credit transfer process, see chapter 10, "Solve the Mysteries of Transferring Credits."

The Los Angeles Valley College (California) Career and Transfer Center says, "We have a library of information on careers and colleges as well as computer access to the World Wide Web. We provide opportunities to meet with college

TIMELINE FOR INCOMING COMMUNITY COLLEGE STUDENTS

Cowley County Community College (Kansas) distributes "transfer tips" at orientation for its freshmen. The material includes this timeline for students who plan to transfer. If you're entering or already at a community college, your personal timetable may vary, but this one presents a well-organized, logical chronology.

FRESHMAN YEAR

Now that you are enrolled for fall classes, it is time to think about which school you may want to transfer to. Although the associate's degrees are designed to transfer to a four-year college, it is important that you know by the beginning of your sophomore year what school you wish to transfer to. That way you can be sure to begin taking the electives that your four-year institution will require.

Spend this time deciding on which schools you are interested in. Be sure to keep in mind that it is more important to select a school that has your major than to select a school just because you like it or just because a friend does—this may be good for you now, but it's your future.

Spend time in the Career Center or visiting with your advisor, family, friends, etc. to determine which schools you may wish to investigate further.

SOPHOMORE YEAR

September: Compile a preliminary list of potential four-year colleges by studying catalogs available in the Career Center and by doing research on the Internet. Contact those schools which interest you via e-mail, telephone, in writing, or through a visit. Be sure to ask for information on your chosen academic program, financial aid, scholarships, and an application for admission.

October: Narrow down your potential schools to your top three choices. Plan a campus visit to those schools over the next two months by contacting the admissions offices there.

November: Continue going on campus visits. Contact instructors and others who can write letters of recommendation on your behalf. Be sure to send them a thank-you note.

December: Start sending in applications for admissions. Be sure to pay attention to deadlines, and make copies for your records. Also, remember that many schools have application fees and will not process your application until the fee has been paid. Begin working on any essays that may be required when applying for scholarships.

January: Finalize any scholarship essays and mail them with the scholarship applications and recommendation letters. Contact the four-year schools to confirm that your applications for admissions were received. Arrange any additional campus tours, if necessary.

February: Apply for financial aid. Contact the four-year schools to confirm that your scholarship applications were received.

March: Contact the four-year schools to confirm that your financial aid file is complete. If not, provide whatever paperwork is necessary as soon as possible. Failure to do this could mean missing out on financial aid and scholarships. Once you know where you have been accepted and what scholarships you have been granted, you are ready to make a financial choice on which school to attend.

April: Obtain an unofficial copy of your transcript to take with you on transfer day. Attend your college's transfer enrollment day. Begin checking into on- and off-campus housing options. Arrange to have your official community college transcripts sent to your transfer college as soon as you graduate. The sooner the better.

RECOMMENDATIONS FOR COMMUNITY COLLEGE TRANSFERS

Here are the most important recommendations that community college transfer experts give their own students:

• Visit your target schools

• Apply to more than one college

• Speak with advisors or counselors from the admissions staff at your community college

• Meet with community college faculty members in any field you're considering as majors to discuss your plans

• Submit your application and supporting material early

The most frequent mistakes, they say, include:

• Failing to adequately research requirements at the new school or prospective major

• Taking too narrow a focus on which colleges to transfer to

• Failing to get written confirmation of transfer information you received verbally during a visit, at a college fair, or over the telephone

• Neglecting to submit the application fee

• Waiting until the last minute to apply, thus preventing the college from contacting you in time if something essential is missing from your file

representatives and conduct workshops on such topics as 'How to Transfer,' 'Deciding on a Major,' and 'Application Workshops.' Career counseling, assessment, testing, and information on registration materials for the SAT, ACT, and Law School Admissions Test are also available."

Erin Weller Hitzemann, the transfer services coordinator and educational planner at Green River Community College (Washington), says, "We show [students] how to access transfer guides, help them understand the direct transfer agreement under the associate's of arts program, and connect them with transfer reps at the university."

Green River provides a good illustration of the variety of support services available. Its College Transfer Center offers a collection of catalogs from colleges and universities in the state, application forms and program information, computers for college and scholarship research, and advisors who work specifically with prospective transfer students. It offers a series of transfer-related workshops on such topics as planning your transfer in medical sciences, education, engineering, or business administration; choosing a major, planning a major in alternative medicine; and portfolio development. Portfolio development refers to ways to collect and display a portfolio of your past work—such as drawings, sketches, photographs, poems, or short stories—to show to admissions officers and faculty at a target school. The transfer center, which has its own Web site, also distributes information on recruiter visits and puts on transfer fairs that draw recruiters from most of Washington's four-year institutions. Its newsletter, *Transfer Gazette*, publishes a schedule of upcoming recruiter visits and the dates of open houses at four-year campuses across the state.

Many community colleges organize similar specialized transfer workshops. At Salt Lake Community College (Utah), they include sessions for criminal justice, computer science, nursing, occupational therapy, pharmacy, business, physical therapy, radiology, chemical engineering, civil engineering, predental, teaching, and other fields of study. There also are financial aid workshops.

In closing, don't ignore the expertise of the professional and academic staff at your community college to help you identify and apply to a new school. While these people don't carry the primary responsibility—that's your obligation—they take pride in the successful advancement and transition of their students to four-year institutions. They also have experience and resources that can improve your chances for success, but only if you take advantage of those services.

And it's essential, as counselor Suzanne Woodward of John Wood Community College (Illinois) puts it, to "take personal responsibility for the whole process."

8

THE
APPLICATION
PROCESS

THINK OF THE TRANSFER APPLICATION PROCESS AS

comparable to screening for a better job or a new opportunity. Showcase your achievements and strengths while explaining your weaknesses or failures. "Successful transfer applicants are focused and engaged in their learning process," says Mt. Holyoke College (Massachusetts). The application and its supporting material provide the chance to demonstrate your focus and your engagement in that learning process.

ADMISSIONS EXPECTATIONS

Not surprisingly, recruiters look for the best. Says McGill University (Quebec): "Applicants must have well-above-average academic records and prerequisites appropriate to the program they wish to pursue." Although colleges are eager to add transfer students to their ranks—especially those with superior qualifications, special talents, unusual determination, or a clear drive to succeed—you are competing for a finite number of openings.

The more competitive and highly ranked the school, the tougher the contest. It's essential that you don't make mistakes in the application process. To use a phrase from Arthur Miller's Pulitzer Prize–winning play, *Death of a Salesman*, you won't be judged "on a smile and a shoeshine." Instead, shine at every step—from the fill-in-the-blanks section of the application to the recommendations, essays, portfolio, interviews, and supplemental material you submit.

Also, remember that you're being evaluated differently than high school seniors because you've previously gone through the application process and enrolled in

"Competition for transfer openings has increased in recent years. Thus, strong academic preparation and performance are primary elements in our admission decisions."

—University of California at Los Angeles

at least one other college. The expectation is even greater that you'll do it right this time.

At the same time, though, your high school record may come into play, no matter how well you're doing at your current institution. In many instances, that's because you've finished less than one or two years of college before transferring. For example, the University of Connecticut evaluates transfer applicants on a combination of high school (grades, class rank, and ACT or SAT scores) and college work to date unless they've finished at least two years of college. Rowan University (New Jersey) looks at high school transcripts and test scores for students who will have twenty-four or fewer credits completed when they arrive.

Some colleges always review your high school record. Here's the rationale at Vassar College (New York): "Since the competition is highly competitive, an applicant's entire academic history is considered in the admission process, and we require high school records with the application. It is difficult for students who have had an unsuccessful high school career to be competitive applicants. However, as the distance from an applicant's high school years grows, the weight assigned to that performance is lessened."

Each institution has its own academic and nonacademic criteria for evaluating transfer applicants. On the academic level, they typically include number of credits completed, college GPA, and progress toward your intended major. In addition, colleges may allow their admissions staff to exercise discretion by considering such factors as employment and family obligations, as well as your past and future involvement in extracurricular activities.

There may be more than one set of standards imposed by a school. For example, Chapman University (California) considers transfer applicants with a minimum GPA of 2.5 if they would have qualified for admission as a high school senior and are in good standing at their current institution. Applicants who wouldn't have qualified straight from high school must complete at least twenty-four transferable credits with the same minimum 2.5 GPA be considered.

Beyond the formal academic and nonacademic criteria, a college may give preference to applicants from community and junior colleges with which they have articulation agreements. Those are contracts governing the transfer of credits among two-year and four-year schools.

What if you want to stay within the same system but attend a different four-year campus? Multicampus systems sometimes have expedited procedures to handle such requests. For example, if you're already enrolled at one campus in the University of South Carolina system and want to switch to another, you're not regarded as a transfer student; instead, you use a change-of-campus form available at your current campus. Similarly, if you're enrolled in a degree program at one Indiana University campus, you can use an intercampus transfer procedure instead of applying for readmission.

Please note that this doesn't mean there are no standards for approval. An intercampus transfer to Indiana University at Bloomington, the star of that state's system, requires a minimum 2.0 GPA, with tougher requirements for particular majors. And if you didn't meet admission standards for the Bloomington campus when you finished high school, you'll need to complete at least twelve credit hours at your present Indiana University campus.

Some multicampus systems don't operate that way, however. At the University of California at Los Angeles, for instance, intercampus transfers within the University of California system aren't automatic. Instead, you vie for space with all other transfer applicants.

NOT ALL MAJORS ARE CREATED EQUAL

When it comes to selecting a major or program within a university, not all are treated the same during the transfer admissions process. Your choice of majors can affect the acceptance decision. It can tip the balance in your favor if you

"Keep Murphy's Law in mind and photocopy everything you need—we all rely on an imperfect postal system."

—Washington University (Missouri)

"Students who knowingly falsify transcripts or test scores or who fail to indicate all previously attended institutions will be denied admission to, or will be disenrolled from, the university."

—University of Colorado at Denver

already took specific courses or opt for a low-demand major. Alternatively, it could tip the scales against you if you haven't yet taken certain courses or prefer a popular major. The GPA threshold for transfer can vary as well.

A college may classify certain majors as "impacted" because of high demand that outpaces the number of available slots. That makes competition more rugged, so the college may demand a higher GPA as well as completion of all preparatory courses before admission. The list varies from institution to institution and over time, but high-demand majors often include business administration, education, pharmacy, nursing, communications, sociology, biology, and economics.

When you narrow the field of target schools, pay careful attention to the application requirements—or at least strong suggestions—for your intended major. If you can't meet them, applying may waste your time, energy, and money. Here are five examples of the requirements for would-be transfers to popular majors at the University of California at Los Angeles:

- *Music history:* one year of music theory and one year of introductory courses in music history
- *Atmospheric, oceanic, and environmental sciences:* one year each of calculus and calculus-based physics with lab; one general chemistry course; and C++ or FORTRAN programming
- *English:* one course each in expository writing and critical reading and writing; a one-year survey of English literature; and two years of one foreign language or a combination of courses in foreign language and literature
- *Psychology:* one course each in introductory psychology, physical anthropol-

ogy, introductory philosophy, and statistics; biology with lab; introductory physics with lab; and introductory chemistry with lab

- *Economics:* critical reading and writing; one course each in microeconomics, statistics, and macroeconomics; and two courses in calculus

Similarly, the University of Northern Iowa recommends that would-be transfers to its communicative disorders major arrive with courses in linguistics, anthropology, sociology, and psychology. Prospective finance majors should have taken principles of accounting, principles of macroeconomics and microeconomics, and introductory courses in information systems, business statistics, and decision techniques. And geography transfers are encouraged to have completed courses in human, world, and physical geography, introductory cartography, and quantitative methods in spatial analysis.

As for grades, school requirements vary. At West Virginia University, a minimum GPA of 2.0 is necessary for arts and sciences, engineering and mineral resources, physical education, creative arts, as well as for most agriculture and forestry majors. But business and economics hopefuls need at least a 2.75 GPA, while education and pre–speech pathology and audiology applicants need a 3.0. And for landscape architecture, the threshold varies by semester: 2.25 for fall transfers and 2.5 for spring transfers.

And at Hawaii Pacific University, transfer applicants generally need a GPA of at least 2.0, but would-be marine biology, oceanography, and environmental science majors need at least a 2.5 in prior math and science courses for normal transfer admission. At the University of Missouri in Columbia, students interested in agriculture, food, and natural resources majors need a 2.0 GPA for acceptance, unless they want agricultural economics, which requires a minimum 2.5.

THREE APPLICATION PRINCIPLES

Keep these three principles in mind throughout the application process:

BE HONEST

Don't lie. Ever. Adverse information may embarrass you but doesn't inevitably doom your application to the shredder. Texas Christian University asks transfer

TRANSFER STUDENTS' RIGHTS AND RESPONSIBILITIES

You must complete all materials that are required for application and submit your application on or before the published deadlines. You should be the sole author of your application.

You have the right to receive information from colleges and universities about their transfer admission requirements, including all documents required for admission, housing, and comprehensive information about their institutions' costs, aid opportunities, practices, and packaging policies.

You have the right to receive information about transfer of courses, credit hours, quality points, and degree requirements. This includes information about transferring courses with grades below a C, courses you may have repeated, and credit previously granted by examination or advance placement.

You should know that admission officers at National Association for College Admission Counseling member institutions will not recruit students who are currently enrolled at other institutions unless those students initiate the inquiries, or unless institutions that provide transfer programs seek such cooperation.

You have the responsibility to research and understand the transfer policies and procedures of each college and university to which you plan to apply, including admission, financial aid, scholarships, and housing. This includes being aware of any deadlines, restrictions and other transfer criteria. You also have to be sure that you understand the policies of each college or university regarding deposits that you may be required to make before you enroll.

—National Association for College Admission Counseling

applicants if they're ineligible to return to any former college—generally due to suspension or expulsion. But the application adds, "Disclosure does not automatically disqualify you for consideration for admission, but will initiate a review by appropriate university officials."

If you get caught lying or omitting information, you'll be punished. If you don't get caught, you'll worry that you will get caught. Fraud is most commonly committed by altering transcripts and grade reports, forging recommendations, or misrepresenting your state of residence to qualify for lower tuition at a public college. And even if a lie isn't detected while the application is under review, it may well be discovered during your years at the new college, when you apply to graduate school, or when you seek a job.

As the British Columbia Institute of Technology explains bluntly: "It is a serious offense to submit fraudulent documents when applying for admission/registration. This includes submission of information constituting misrepresentation. Applicants who submit fraudulent documents will be dealt with severely, with the minimum penalty being non-enrollment for one year and the maximum penalty being an indefinite ban on enrollment."

That type of stigma can haunt you throughout your career.

Omitting embarrassing or unfavorable information also constitutes dishonesty.

BE COMPLETE

Admissions is a competitive process, so failure to fill in all the blanks or submit all required material on time can delay or even block a decision. Especially with rolling admissions, your college of choice may fill its quota of transfer acceptances before you get around to providing the missing information. Rolling admissions is a first-come, first-served process in which admissions staff review applications as they're completed and make decisions without waiting for the application deadline to expire.

You're responsible for your own application. And although the college may notify you if it hasn't received all the necessary information, that may not leave you much time to collect and submit the material.

"Students who fail to acknowledge attendance at any college in which they have been registered automatically waive the right to have that work considered for transfer credit and may be subject to denial of admission, loss of course credit, and/or suspension."

—University of Connecticut

Be aware that completeness includes an explanation for any gaps in your record, particularly embarrassing ones. For guidance on how to deal with such situations, see chapter 9, "Support Your Application."

BE CLEAR

Think professionally. Be sure your application is clear, both in content and in presentation. An unreadable phone number or illegible, handwritten name may prevent an admissions officer from calling one of your references or a past employer.

As Washington University (Missouri) tells prospective transfer students, "Type or clearly print the application. Unfortunately, misspelled or misread names, addresses, and social security numbers often end up as lost files."

ESSENTIAL ELEMENTS OF THE TRANSFER APPLICATION

Be sure to fill out the proper application. Many colleges have a special transfer application. Others use the same application as for high school seniors, with or without a transfer student supplement. There may be a supplemental form for particular programs and majors. At some colleges, specific programs such as business or pharmacy may require you to already have earned a minimum number of credits to apply directly to that program.

Find out whether your target colleges, public or private, participate in a common application process. If so, that simplifies the work if you're seeking admission to more than one participating school. Texas, for instance, uses a common application for transfer students seeking admission to any public university in the state. Students designate which colleges they want the application to go to and pay the fee for each. Participating schools, however, may want you to complete a shorter application of their own, such as one requiring an essay.

The form of an application varies from school to school, but these are the most common types of questions you'll find:

- *Name:* Provide your full name as it appears on any test scores, transcripts, social security card, or other documents and records that the college may consult.

- *Birth date:* Age discrimination is illegal, but some admissions officers feel older transfers are generally more mature, self-motivated, and financially responsible. The birth date also allows colleges to double-check that you are who you claim to be.

- *Gender:* Colleges that accept federal funds cannot discriminate on the basis of gender.

- *Permanent address and phone number:* This is important for two principal reasons. First, it may determine whether or not you qualify for a lower in-state or in-district tuition rate. Second, some colleges strive for geographic diversity among their students, so a selective East Coast school may give added weight to an applicant from the South, while a large urban college may give preference to transfer applicants from a farming area in a distant corner of its state.

- *Current address and phone number:* "Current" means more than today. This address should be good for the next several months because that's where the admissions and financial aid offices will mail things to you.

- *E-mail address:* If you don't have an e-mail account, maybe through your current school, get one from an Internet provider. Many, including Hotmail, Yahoo, and Juno, are free so you don't need to pay a monthly charge to a service like America Online.

- *Citizenship:* This is important for such matters as student visas, eligibility for financial aid, part-time employment, and developing a diverse student body. Noncitizens with permanent resident status may need to provide their permanent resident card number. If you're already in the United States, the college may ask for a copy of your I-94 form from the Immigration and Naturalization Service.

- *Date of high school graduation:* This tells the admissions office how long you've been out of high school and makes it easier to verify high school transcripts.

- *Beginning with your current college, list in order the names and locations of colleges and high schools you've attended:* This section usually requires the name and address of each institution and the dates of attendance. It enables the admissions office to track your educational progress chronologically.

- *Will you complete a degree before you enroll in the new college?* This is one measure of your academic progress and may affect how many credit hours will transfer.

- *Are you eligible to return to all former institutions?* (In other words, have you been suspended, expelled, or placed on academic or disciplinary probation?) Most colleges won't take you as a transfer student if this answer is no. Kenyon College (Ohio) states directly: "Students on suspension from or ineligible to return to a college for academic or social reasons will not be admitted."

- *List employers and employment dates for the last two years:* The college may use this information to account for time gaps in your educational history. Work experience may also suggest life experiences that could factor into the acceptance decision.

- *Family information:* The application may ask for the names, addresses, phone numbers, and occupations of your parents, whether they have postsecondary education, and the names of colleges they've attended. Similarly, it may request the names, ages, schools, and educational levels of your brothers and sisters. Colleges use this information in several ways. For example, some strive to provide extra opportunities to applicants who are the first in their families to attend college. Also, alumni connections—often called "legacies"—

may work in your favor during the review process, especially if you're teetering on the border. Some colleges offer reduced tuition to spouses and children of alumni.

- *Academic record:* The typical application wants your high school rank and the size of your graduating class; your PSAT, SAT, or ACT scores, and your current college grade point average and scale. Be accurate because it's easy for the college to double-check all this information against transcripts and test score reports.

- *Foreign languages in high school:* Some colleges have foreign language requirements to graduate. Your high school work may meet some or all of those requirements, although you may need to take a placement test during orientation or after you arrive on campus.

- *Current courses:* These won't appear on the latest transcript. They also indicate some of your areas of interest and, in some instances, the difficulty of the classes you're now taking.

- *Other college credit possibilities:* This is where you list Advanced Placement, overseas study, studies while in the military, correspondence courses, and other accomplishments that may entitle you to credit toward the requirements at the new college.

- *Intended major or field of study:* What academic areas do you intend to pursue at the college?

- *Career goals:* This is a chance to relate your proposed studies to long-term

"Each applicant is treated as an individual, and personal qualities and experiences are recognized for admission consideration. A well-written essay, a strong recommendation, and extracurricular involvement can make a difference in the selection process, but will not compensate for inadequate academic preparation."

—University of San Diego (California)

APPLICATION REMINDERS

- Check the timetable. When is your transfer application due? There may be earlier deadlines for highly competitive programs or majors. International transfer applicants may face earlier deadlines due to the extra time needed to evaluate foreign course work and to issue nonimmigrant visas.
- When will the admissions office notify you of its decision? And if you're accepted, how long will you have after that to notify the college whether or not you'll attend?
- How about the financial aid application? Verify and meet the submission deadline for the college's financial aid process, as well as the requirements for filing the U.S. Department of Education's Free Application for Federal Student Aid (FAFSA). Carefully read the chapters about financial aid, chapters 11 and 12.
- Keep photocopies of every document you mail in—the application, financial aid form, essays, recommendations, portfolio, and other material.
- File early. Don't push the deadline.
- Give your references ample time to write your recommendations.
- Order high school and college transcripts early. Remember, it's up to you to verify that they've arrived at the college.
- If you lose or can't find an essential form, immediately check the college's Web site because many of them are available online. If not, promptly call or e-mail the admissions office—or drop in if the college is nearby—for a replacement.

goals after you finish school, especially if you can't incorporate this information into your essay or recommendations.

- *Graduate or professional study plans:* These may well change over the next few years but indicate long-term ambitions. This information also helps admissions officers evaluate how your intended majors can help you achieve that goal.

- *ROTC interest:* Are you considering the Reserve Officers Training Corps and, if so, is it for the army, navy, or air force?

- *Academic and extracurricular honors:* Recognition for past accomplishments— in classes, on teams, in community groups, or with campus organizations— provide insights into your interests and abilities, beyond the bare numbers of GPAs and test scores.

- *Recommendations and references:* List the names and relationships of those people who will write your recommendations.

- *Test of English as a Foreign Language (TOEFL):* International students whose native language isn't English will need to indicate if they already have taken the TOEFL and, if not, when they intend to do so.

- *The college itself:* Typical questions ask how you learned about the school and whether you've visited or intend to visit. You may be asked whether you've had contact with a coach, alum, or faculty member; whether you've visited campus or attended an off-campus recruitment event; whether a counselor or academic advisor referred you; or whether the admissions office or a department had invited you to apply.

- *Veteran status:* The college can use this information in several ways. It may explain a time gap in your educational record, signal the availability of benefits to help cover your education costs, indicate a higher level of maturity than other transfer applicants of your age, or suggest the possibility of granting credit based on military experience, training, and course work.

- *Racial, ethnic, and religious information:* You have the legal right not to answer these questions, and the application should clearly state that these questions are optional. Under federal law, this information cannot be required and cannot be the basis of discrimination by the college. However, the institution can use it to improve or refine its recruitment techniques and to design culturally appropriate services for its students.

- *Disabilities:* The application may ask whether you want special consideration based on a disability. This is an optional question. If you answer yes, the

TEN MOST COMMON—AND AVOIDABLE—MISTAKES

Admissions officers see some of the same mistakes over and over again, goofs that can delay or doom approval of your application. Here are ten of the most common—and avoidable—ones:

• Failing to provide enough explanation of your activities—merely listing titles without description—on your application

• Missing deadlines for applications, transcripts, and recommendations

• Failing to list all previous institutions, and to order transcripts from each

• Waiting too long to file for financial aid

• Failing to adequately *understand* your motives for transferring

• Failing to adequately *explain* your reasons for transferring

• Being too narrowly focused or choosing too narrow an academic program

• Lacking a solid understanding of the target college's mission and philosophy

• Failing to write a good essay

• Ignoring the additional requirements and separate deadlines for some majors and programs

college may ask for supporting documentation and should keep that information confidential. The Americans with Disabilities Act prohibiting disabilities-related discrimination applies to colleges.

Individual colleges and college systems may ask other questions as well. The common application for the Florida state system adds optional questions about family obligations that may keep applicants from participating in extracurricular activities, about family household income, and about the number of people in an applicant's household. University College of Cape Breton (Nova Scotia) asks applicants about their mother tongue: English, French, or Mi'kmaq.

APPLICATION FEES

Application fees are nonrefundable and are intended to both cover at least part of the college's admissions office expenses and to deter frivolous applications. It's unusual for a college not to charge a fee, but some waive the transfer fee if you apply by a specified deadline, if you now attend a community or junior college it has an articulation agreement with, or if there is financial need.

Fees vary, and most fall in the $25 to $50 range. Some colleges charge more, and a few impose lower, nominal processing fees. You may be able to pay by credit card, especially if you use the option of applying online.

WHILE YOU'RE WAITING

Don't slack off. Poor performance in your final semester at your present college could short-circuit your transfer plans once the new school sees your final transcript. Also, low grades in current courses might prevent the credits from transferring, affect eligibility for a merit-based scholarship, or preclude the course from counting as a prerequisite.

After working hard to identify target schools, study their offerings and services, visit their campuses, and talk to their admissions staff and professors, it would be a shame to waste that time and effort by messing up the actual application process. Take pride in yourself and what you can accomplish. Don't get sloppy or careless with so much at stake, because even a small oversight or omission can doom your hopes in a competitive admissions process.

9

SUPPORT
YOUR
APPLICATION

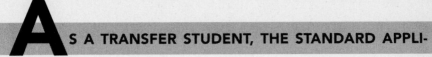

AS A TRANSFER STUDENT, THE STANDARD APPLI-

cation form is only the starting point. No two schools evaluate transfer candidates exactly the same way, but each takes into consideration supplementary information and material, primarily recommendations, essays, test scores, portfolios, and transcripts. Whether required or optional, supplementary information can prove decisive in a college's decision-making process. The closer you balance on the dividing line between acceptance and rejection, the more crucial each element may be.

It's important to remember that there are opportunities for you to emphasize strengths that can offset weaknesses. Say the first-year grades at your current college are below—perhaps significantly below—what your target school expects. Instead of letting the transcript speak bleakly for itself and dooming your chances, make sure that at least one of your recommendations, an essay, or a cover letter explains your previous poor academic performance and puts it in context while offering plausible reasons to believe future performance levels will be higher. Similarly, your portfolio of art or writing may tangibly demonstrate skills and talents that formal grades may not reflect.

The University of California at Los Angeles explains its approach to such personal criteria this way, and suggests explaining such information in your personal statement or essay:

"We also consider the presence of circumstances that may have prevented students from achieving their highest overall academic performance:

• Full- or part-time employment while attending school

• Family responsibility

• Students returning to school, where early grades are not indicative of the strong academic performance demonstrated in recent course work

• Ongoing involvement in clubs, campus organizations, student government, or community service."

ESSAYS

The essay is a marketing tool and a sales device. Frankly, you're the product, and the admissions office is the customer. If you don't go through an interview, the essay may be your only chance to display your personality and way of thinking in your own words, without the filter of a transcript, fill-in-the-blank application, or recommendations from past instructors. If you do go through an interview, the essay will supplement the personal rapport you hopefully created and provide another benchmark for evaluating your ability to communicate and organize.

It's actually tougher to write short and tight than to write long and loose, but admissions committees look for control as well as clarity and content. Follow maximum length guidelines or limits. Some applications impose a strict ceiling on the number of words, while others leave it up to you. Don't waste valuable words—or pad an essay that's not fully thought out—by repeating the question, even in slightly modified words. Coe College (Iowa) advises, "It should be the length of a *good* story."

Show, don't show off.

Start strong. Think of the lead—your opening paragraph or paragraphs—as a storefront window and imagine busy admissions officers walking briskly down the street. They'll glance into each window as they pass by, but few of the displays will compel them to stop and linger, let alone walk inside to shop. When it comes to reading essays, they can immediately sense what is trite, what is stale, what is boring, what is inarticulate, and what is inaccurate. If your essay is to have impact, it must start in a compelling enough way to intrigue the reviewer to read to the end. And it should demonstrate a compelling reason to put you on the short list for acceptance.

Avoid pretentious words and ornate, flowery, and stilted prose. Use plain English. Obey the rules of spelling and grammar. Subjects need predicates. Sentences need proper punctuation. Singular nouns need singular pronouns and verbs. Avoid sexist terminology. Avoid empty words like very and really.

Draft, edit, rewrite, and rewrite again. Proofread carefully, both on the screen and on paper. Use—but don't rely on—the spell-check program on your computer. The software won't tell you whether you chose the right word, only whether whatever word you chose is spelled correctly.

PERSPECTIVE: A DEAN OF ADMISSION TALKS ABOUT ESSAYS

The essays may seem especially daunting. What do they want, you ask; what are they looking for?

We honestly do not have hidden answers to the questions we ask. Quite simply, we seek an accurate reflection in these papers of the person you are. We ask that you be true to the person you have already become, and tell us about that individual. You may feel that your interests and activities up to now don't amount to much. Or you may feel that they are significant, but you don't want to brag. Try to find a middle ground. We ask you to recognize what you have already accomplished. For example, in choosing to apply to only a few colleges, you have made a series of significant choices. What does that show about your values? What other choices have you made in your life guided by similar instincts, or by a wish for excitement and challenge? Answer those questions, and you have the seed of a fine essay or two.

You can learn a great deal about yourself in this process. Notice what comes to mind as you weigh your life experiences. Write about those that seem important to you. We, too, will be persuaded that they are important. Experience alone is not enough. We want to know what insight you have gained from your experience. Your own learning and growth lie at the heart of a good essay. Above all, remember that these essays are about you and deserve your best effort.

—Thyra Briggs, dean of admission, Sarah Lawrence College (New York)

TYPICAL ESSAY QUESTIONS

These are examples of the types of questions you may find on your transfer applications. And if you're allowed to write on any topic of interest, these will suggest approaches that may work for you in tackling the assignment:

• "Outline your reasons for leaving your most recent college and applying for transfer. . . ."

—Washington University (Missouri)

• "Tell us something else we should know to understand you better. This might include a person, experience, issue, idea, value, or topic of your choice. If you were out of school for more than a year, describe that experience and its impact. If you are not enrolled in school now, please explain."

—Wesleyan University (Connecticut)

• "Discuss a recent scientific advance and the important legal, ethical, or philosophical questions it raises."

—Sarah Lawrence College (New York)

• "Explain the role that academic integrity has played in your life."

—Miami University (Florida)

• "There are limitations to what grades, scores, and recommendations can tell us about any applicant. We ask you to write a personal essay that will help us to know you better. In the past, candidates have written about their families, intellectual and extracurricular interests, ethnicity or culture, school and community events to which they have had strong reactions, people who have influenced them, significant experiences, personal aspirations, or topics that spring entirely from their imaginations. There is no 'correct' way to respond to our request. Write about what matters to you, and you are bound to convey a strong sense of who you are."

—Yale University (Connecticut)

• "We ask that you write a one-page artist's statement: an essay, statement of purpose, epic poem, autobiography, dear diary entry, or whatever best reflects your creative process."

—Art Institute of Cincinnati (Ohio)

• "What are your current thoughts about careers and career preparation as they relate to you, whether you are undecided or firmly committed to a specific field?"

—Hope College (Michigan)

• "Imagine that Bryn Mawr College is compiling the stories of past, present, and future alumnae for an anthology called *The Bryn Mawr Book of Women's Lives.* Write a letter to the editor with the purpose of convincing her to include your story in the anthology. Be sure to articulate why your experiences—those which you have had and/or those which you imagine having—would make for compelling reading."

—Bryn Mawr College (Pennsylvania)

• "Why did you choose your present college/university, and why will Bowdoin be better suited to your educational needs?"

—Bowdoin College (Maine)

• "We'd like you to tell us about the parts of your personality that can't be described in your transcript. Maybe you took a trip that changed your view of the world. Or met someone who made you rethink your stereotypes. People, places, books, activities—if it's helped make you who you are, we'd like to hear about it."

—Coe College (Iowa)

• "Tell us about an opinion you've had to defend or an incident in your life which placed you in conflict with the beliefs of a majority of people and explain how this affected your value system."

—Massachusetts Institute of Technology

• "According to Stephen Carter, we can admire those with integrity even if we disagree with them. Are there people you admire even though you deeply disagree with them? What do you admire about them? How do you reconcile this apparent contradiction in your assessment?"

—Duke University (North Carolina)

While your essay should be well honed, it also should sound like a person of your age and experience wrote it. One concern that's been raised about online essay critique services—companies that charge a fee—is that they sometimes overpolish an applicant's work so the tone sounds stilted and artificial rather than like the genuine person you are.

Ask somebody you respect to review your essay before you mail or e-mail it. It may be a counselor, advisor, or professor at your current school, even a friend who's a skilled writer. You want their reaction to substance and style, as well as corrections of any grammar and spelling goofs that slipped past you.

For some colleges, you'll find essays tailored to particular programs and majors. At the University of the Arts (Pennsylvania) transfer applicants for the communication program can select from among three options, including "Choose a current advertising campaign for a nationally known (branded) product. Write a critique of the campaign, identifying what you find most effective or ineffective in the presentation, what social groups the campaign targets, and how you would change the campaign."

As with everything you write, remember your audience. Here, it will be admissions officers—generally in their twenties, thirties, or forties—who have read thousands of essays. They've seen the good, the bad, the ugly, and the ugliest. When it comes to content, you need to connect with admissions people. Be sincere.

The novelist Mary McCarthy once observed, "We are all heroes of our own story." If you carry that concept into writing an application essay or personal statement, you'll see that the topic and approach must matter to you, and the presentation must reflect that you do care. While some colleges give you a topic, or let you select from a few, others leave it open-ended, inviting you simply to write about something that matters to you. Some applicants find that a tougher, more challenging assignment than merely writing about a topic selected by the college.

Does the topic need to be dramatic or earth shaking? No, but it must be meaningful. If an experience or event is significant enough to write about, show in reality the questions don't follow. Details are far more important than generalities. As you can see from the sample questions, some colleges allow great leeway to explore a subject that concerns or interests you. Don't waste the opportunity.

As for the tone of your writing, make it appropriate for the chosen topic and approach. Be careful about humor—it's hard to pull off successfully and it's easy to turn off a reviewer.

Also be sure your tone and topic are consistent with the college's philosophy, values, and self-defined mission. "We look for a well-constructed essay that shows writing capabilities that we consider very strong," explains Myron Burney, an admissions counselor at Morehouse College (Georgia). "We look for content to see if you have a goal in mind, to see what the applicant brings to our institution. We want to know he's done some research on Morehouse."

In reviewing a transfer applicant's file, Burney continues, "We want to know they have a plan. In most cases, well over 50 percent, the essay will speak high volumes about their goal, their vision, and their commitment."

Vanderbilt University (Tennessee) doesn't dictate the topic for what it calls the "personal statement" but counsels, "Your essay should allow us to develop a sense of your effectiveness in written communication and to understand more fully who you are and what you value." The essay, it adds, is a "great opportunity to communicate a personal perspective to the admissions committee."

St. John's College (Maryland and New Mexico) offers these insights into how it reads and evaluates essays: "The set of reflective essays that forms the core of our application is important to the Admissions Committee, but we do not expect perfection, and we are not looking for highly polished pieces of formal prose. Instead, we want you to write about yourself as fully and freely as you can, assessing your formal education and personal experiences and telling us why you think St. John's is the appropriate next step."

It continues, reassuringly, "What you write will be read carefully, but sympathetically, by a group of teaching faculty and the director of admissions. You should take the essays seriously, but not too seriously. We hope you will see them as an opportunity to articulate for yourself where you have been and what you expect out of a college education, and we hope you will enjoy writing them."

RECOMMENDATIONS

The recommendation is a tool intended to provide admissions staff with an outside interpretation of your past performance, future potential, and personality. There are cases when a recommendation makes the difference between acceptance and rejection, although in general you can expect your previous academic performance and essays to weigh more heavily. The recommendation should give a professional evaluation of your social and academic skills and go beyond what your transcript already shows.

Therefore, the most meaningful and most effective recommendations come from people who know you well, people who can speak in specifics and not trite platitudes. That's one incentive for developing close relationships with faculty and becoming involved in extracurricular activities at your current college. As Myron Burney, the Morehouse College admissions counselor, puts it, "We become leery" when the recommendation doesn't come from a professor who has taught the applicant.

A professor you had in a twenty-student creative writing seminar or foreign language lab is more likely to fill your needs than the one who taught your two hundred–student introductory economics or biology lecture course—even if you received a lower grade in the seminar than in the lecture course.

Each college's application packet or Web page will explain whom the recommendations must come from. For transfer students, it might call for one from your current advisor or dean on behalf of your present college, plus another from somebody who knows you well enough to attest to your intellectual and personal promise, such as a professor, employer, coach, clergy member, or neighbor. The college may require an academic recommendation from an instructor who has taught you for at least one full semester.

In some instances, an alternative to a faculty member is acceptable. The Art Academy of Cincinnati (Ohio) will consider a recommendation from a professional artist with whom you've worked. It might substitute for one from a professor.

Don't shop around for a recommendation from somebody with perceived clout—such as a politician, trustee, or generous benefactor of the college—who can't speak sincerely and personally about your qualifications and character. Admissions officers are astute enough to discount or disregard such letters. It's one thing to *earn* a recommendation from the state senator you interned with, but there's little value in an endorsement simply based on the fact you're a constituent or your parents donated money to the lawmaker's campaign.

Some of the material requested in recommendations is routine, such as your grade point average and class rank.

One section typically asks for an evaluation of these types of characteristics: academic ability and scholarship; academic motivation; energy and initiative; originality; leadership; self-confidence; personality; curiosity; expression of ideas; cooperativeness; concern for others; analytical ability; courtesy; maturity; health; independence; participation; willingness to admit error; acceptance of constructive criticism; and integrity. The person then ranks each characteristic

"Your personal essay is our opportunity to get to know you better. Please be candid and share with us information that will help us understand you and see the whole picture of your life—including and beyond academics."

—Seton Hall University (New Jersey)

along this type of scale: below average; average; good; excellent; outstanding; or no basis for judgment.

Here's another kind of scale you might encounter: "Considering all qualifications, I believe the applicant will: do superior work; do above-average work; do average work; encounter some difficulty; or have significant difficulty."

The most valuable part of the recommendation comes through answers to such open-ended questions as:

- "In what ways might you distinguish the student's academic performance from other able students?"

- "Either through personal experience or in talking with others, how would you characterize this student's level of intellectual curiosity and approach to learning?"

- "Are there any factors that might interfere with the candidate's academic performance and/or personal relationships?"

- "Describe any other unusual accomplishments or personal circumstances that we should know about this student."

- "We are interested in whatever you feel is important for us to know. Anecdotes and specific illustrations are useful."

Here, the content and quality of the response outweigh mere length. Examples, specifics, and anecdotes are most persuasive, and realism counts more than hype.

Admissions officers say they use the answers to assess such factors as a transfer applicant's level of engagement with academic material, ability to handle assignments, level of seriousness and maturity, and productivity.

Religion-affiliated colleges may require a recommendation from a member of the clergy. One of them, Asbury College (Kentucky), asks pastors to describe applicants' "willingness to cooperate well with his/her peers and with those in authority," dependability, church participation, and use of alcohol, drugs, or tobacco. It also asks whether the minister has had the chance to observe the applicants "being honest and fair" and whether the applicants "understand and will be able to adjust to a Christian community environment."

Occasionally, you'll come across a college that requires a work recommendation as well. For Wheelock College (Massachusetts), it must come from a "supervisor of some work situation," whether paid or volunteer, who is asked about the specific job you performed, your "major emotional and social strengths, your maturity and concern for others, and your effectiveness in carrying out work responsibilities."

In addition, a college may offer, as does the University of San Diego (California), to look at optional personal recommendations that supplement but don't replace the required ones. Williams College (Massachusetts) calls them "optional peer references" completed by a friend or somebody else appropriate. Associate admissions director Frances Lapidus says, "It gives us another view of the person and brings the person more into focus."

When I'm solicited for a recommendation, I always ask my students about their future plans and require a résumé and copies of some of their written work, even if I've had them recently in class, so my comments will be as complete and accurate as possible. As a transfer applicant, provide that type of information to everyone you seek a recommendation from. It is also courteous to provide an addressed, stamped envelope.

It's *your* obligation to ensure that recommendations arrive by the deadline, so give people as much advance notice as possible so theirs can be done thoughtfully and on time.

SAMPLE RECOMMENDATION

Here are excerpts from an actual transfer recommendation considered highly effective by the admissions officers who reviewed it. You'll see how the writer, who is a community college chemistry professor, used specific information to flesh out general observations about the applicant. Rather than gloss over problems and failures, the writer explained each situation and how the student overcame—or is overcoming—them. As a result, the recommendation is by no means a form letter. Instead, it provides valuable insights to the real decision makers, the admissions staff.

I became acquainted with her during the 1999–2000 academic year when she was enrolled in my general and inorganic I and II chemistry courses. I have continued to see her and had opportunities to converse with her about her progress in her subsequent classes since that time. It is a real pleasure to write this recommendation for this talented, compassionate, confident young woman.

She came as a very young student and has successfully combined a heavy academic load with a job and responsibility caring for younger siblings with special needs.

When I first met her, she exhibited behavior that was typical for a student who sat in the front row. She came to class prepared and on time, worked quietly by herself on problems, and asked questions privately after class. As she became more comfortable with my teaching style and the students, she became a leader in the class. I would see her lean over to explain something to another student or raise her hand to ask a question that one of her classmates was too shy to ask. She worked hard and demanded that I meet the challenge of helping her learn. We were both disappointed in the C she earned that first semester because neither of us felt it reflected her learning in the course. I was happy to see that it encouraged her to work even harder in the following semester. She became a fixture during my office hours, and I heard her making arrangements for a study group to meet or found her sitting at the table outside my office working with other students when I returned from class.

During the time I spent with her in my office, I had the opportunity to get to know her. She told me about high school, her family, her job, and her community college experiences. She told me about the issues that concerned her in high school, the joys and concerns of living with younger siblings with special needs, the frustrations of trying to work her way through college, and the excitement of her experience as she plans to study abroad this summer.

She wants to continue her education and become a physician. I know that her drive to learn, her willingness to help other students, and her compassion for individuals who don't fit in will make her an asset to your program.

Detailed letters like this one demonstrate that the writer knows you well enough—flaws and all—for his or her comments to receive serious consideration. That's why the observations of a professor who gave you a less-than-stellar grade but respects your abilities may help more than a routine letter recapping the obvious, even from an instructor who gave you top marks. For the admissions office, familiarity and candor in a recommendation weigh more heavily than generalities and puffery.

CONFIDENTIALITY

Colleges want candid assessments, but some faculty and other people who write recommendations are leery of being too candid lest the student find out. However, federal law—the 1974 Family Educational Rights and Privacy Act—allows applicants who later enroll at a college to inspect and review recommendations as long as they're in the file. (That doesn't affect applicants who are rejected or who choose not to attend, because they have no legal right of access.) Some schools routinely destroy all recommendations after a fixed period.

Some applications ask the *students* whether or not they want to waive that right of access and agree not to look at their recommendations—a choice that shouldn't affect whether or not you get in. Some applications ask the *person writing the recommendation* whether it should be kept on file or removed after the application process ends.

INTERVIEWS

Should you interview? Some colleges strongly recommend an interview, and one may be required for particular programs or under certain circumstances, such as an interruption of your education for a year or longer. Even where they're optional, they may play a role in the admissions decision.

"You don't HAVE to come in for an interview (we don't require one) but we'd really like you to. We pay close attention when students come in and talk to us about their achievements and the obstacles they have faced. An interview could improve your chances of admittance."

—University of Massachusetts at Lowell

Not all interviews are held on campus, thus making it easier for you to undergo one without traveling a long distance to the school. Check with the admissions office about arranging an interview off-campus with a traveling admissions officer, at a college fair in your area, or with alumni who live near you. Some colleges will arrange evening interviews for the applicants' convenience.

Seize the moment. This may be your only face-to-face chance to connect with a decision maker, to ask tough questions, to explain potholes along your past road, to discuss your concerns, to differentiate yourself as an individual from a pool of faceless transfer applicants all competing for a spot. If you don't portray yourself well on paper—in essays and on test scores, for instance—you still can sell yourself in person.

What key factors do admissions staff hope to glean from the interviews? They include your reasons for choosing that school, your level of understanding what's expected in your chosen area of study, a sense of your plans, a feeling for your intellectual curiosity, and an impression of your personal qualities.

At Hilbert College (New York), interviews are required of transfer applicants who seem to have exhibited difficulties at other institutions. Admissions director Harry Gong says, "In cases where an interview is necessary, the counselor tries to make sure that Hilbert can provide the services that a student may need and that the student has the ability to succeed."

And at Keuka College (New York), assistant admissions director Chris Tillman says, "We encourage those on the edge to come in for an interview. Coming in and really selling themselves would jump out in my mind." Michigan State

University also suggests interviews when there are mitigating circumstances, according to associate admissions director Thomas Hoiles: "Too often, an applicant's admissibility may come into question because he or she had difficulty at a previous institution. The interview allows admissions counselors the opportunity to query the applicant, one on one, regarding the causes of that difficulty, thus allowing for a decision based on the best evidence."

Prepare for and make the most of the interview. Don't waste the moment by asking for information that's readily accessible in the catalog or on the Web site. Don't pitch softball questions like "Why are students happy here?" Don't be confrontational, like asking, "Why should I go here when I can transfer to a 'better' college?" Don't be rude or arrogant, but don't brownnose to curry favor. Dress appropriately.

When you schedule the interview, find out how much time you'll have and plan your questions accordingly. Get there early, and give yourself enough time to get to campus, find a parking spot, and walk to the office.

PORTFOLIOS AND AUDITIONS

Some programs require transfer applicants to submit portfolios of their previous creative work or to audition. In other situations a portfolio or audition is an optional but potentially decisive way to boost your chances of acceptance. (Vanderbilt University in Tennessee characterizes the audition for its music school as "a vital consideration" for acceptance. Live rather than taped auditions are usually preferred unless travel distance is prohibitive, and many colleges will schedule them for Saturdays.) This is especially true if you want to major or minor in these fields:

- Studio arts and fine arts such as painting, drawing, or sculpture
- Graphic design or computer-assisted design
- Photography
- Interior design
- Architecture and landscape architecture
- Writing, including creative writing such as playwriting, poetry, and fiction

• Performing arts such as dance, music, and theater

• Journalism, communication, or public relations

• Multimedia

• Fashion design

Depending on the field and college, you may also be asked for a performing arts résumé outlining your performance experience and training, including length of study, studios, dates, and instructors.

Even if you're thinking of fields far removed from this list, a portfolio or audition can highlight some of your skills. They may be academic such as writing—which is essential for any major—or may relate to extracurricular interests like theater, photography, filmmaking, or art that make you a better-rounded candidate. *Be selective.* A portfolio *shouldn't* be a dumping ground for everything you've ever done. To be effective, it *should* highlight the best you've done so far as an indicator of your promise and potential. Pick out pieces you're proudest of. Similarly, an audition—whether live or taped—should accurately reflect your talents, competence, and skills.

The college may tell you how much to submit in your portfolio. That's true at Washington University (Missouri), where architecture transfer applicants are told to provide ten to fifteen pieces "reflecting a variety of work assignments," while art transfers must provide ten to fifteen slides that "show a variety of art experiences, including drawings, work utilizing design principles, and some work in color."

The Art Academy of Cincinnati (Ohio) requires a portfolio of twenty original pieces that demonstrate "strong art-making skills and individual expression." The twenty must include black-and-white observational drawings from life, at least one self-portrait in any medium, and a selection of work in any color medium. Admissions director Mary Jane Zumwalde explains, "The portfolio is the biggest concern of ours. It goes hand in hand with the college GPA."

Your audition may be limited to a maximum amount of time. At Emerson College (Massachusetts), for example, prospective acting majors must come to an audition "prepared with a single monologue you care about. It can be from a contemporary or classical play, and should last no more than two to three minutes."

If there are no guidelines, be reasonable. A writer might submit a dozen poems but only two short stories. A public relations major might submit one media kit developed during an internship rather than bits and pieces of a dozen projects. A musician may include both the score and a tape of an original composition.

Find out as much as possible about *what* the college wants from the audition. The competition for transfer spots can be tough, even brutal, in a top-rated program, and you need every legitimate advantage. Here's what Emerson tells prospective acting majors: "Make sure that you have memorized [your monologue], not by rote but rather through exploration. Recognize that we are not looking for versatility and range at this point. We are looking for honesty and a strong commitment to what you are doing. Choose something that is important to you and try to make us feel and understand what you are sharing with us. At the audition itself, you may be asked to work on this piece improvisationally after you have shared your prepared work." And while Emerson tells musical theater applicants that they may select any two songs they want, it would be wise to follow the college's strong suggestion: "Material from the musical theatre repertoire will be most useful in evaluating you for the program."

"While the presentation of your portfolio needn't be elaborate, it should demonstrate the respect you have for your work. If you show us your portfolio in person, you should be able to talk about it—what each project involved, how you made decisions, what you learned from the experience, and how you feel about your finished piece."

—University of the Arts (Pennsylvania)

"The portfolio is one of the most important elements of your application. It is a great indicator of your readiness for the rigors of the degree program and allows us tremendous insight into your creativity."

—Art Academy of Cincinnati (Ohio)

Be professional. Because a portfolio is intended to showcase your talent, it's acceptable to improve on what you've previously done. For example, if you submit a short story first done for a creative writing course, there's nothing wrong with rewriting it to make it better. Even if you choose not to rewrite, submit only a clean copy—not one with your grade and instructor's comments on it.

Be organized. No admissions counselor or academic reviewer wants to wade through a disorganized stack of papers or pictures, watch an unedited video, or listen to an unedited audiotape of seemingly unconnected clips.

After you pick an appropriate number of pieces, arrange them in a logical order and label them with essential explanatory information. If a poem was published in a campus literary magazine or an article appeared in the college or local newspaper, include the name and date of publication. If your pottery or sketches were displayed at an art show or gallery, include the place and dates. For a video or audiotape, include a written description of where and when the material was recorded.

Write a short introduction to your portfolio, discussing what's in the package, the overall context of your work, and its relevance to your academic, career, or extracurricular plans. Put the material together in a suitable binder labeled with your name, address, phone number, and e-mail. Place any photos or slides in plastic sleeves.

Never submit originals or your only copies, because they may get lost or never be returned. At your request, the college may be willing to arrange for an in-person review of your portfolio, of original works of art, or of performance excerpts during a campus visit.

TEST SCORES

Each target school will tell you what American College Test (ACT) or Scholastic Aptitude Test (SAT) scores from high school it needs. Some demand scores from all transfer applicants, but others want scores only from applicants with fewer than a specified number of credits.

Some colleges exempt transfer applicants twenty-one or twenty-five or older from the test score requirement, even if they have only a handful of credits. Other common exemptions are for military veterans, international students unless they're from Canada, transfer applicants who have been out of high school at least five years, and recipients of associate's or technical degrees.

Incidentally, a growing number of colleges are moving away from mandatory admissions tests, according to a study by the group FairTest. At this point, roughly 20 percent of U.S. universities and colleges no longer require the ACT or SAT for some or all applicants. The shift in attitude reflects several considerations, including concerns about fairness, validity, and ability of those tests to predict success in college. Other colleges are downplaying the weight they give to test results. Instead, admissions offices are taking a more holistic approach and relying more heavily on grades, essays, recommendations, life and work experience, and extracurricular activities.

INTERNATIONAL STUDENTS

If English isn't your first language, you may be required to take the Test of English as a Foreign Language (TOEFL), pass an alternative test offered by the college, or otherwise demonstrate your English fluency to the college's satisfaction. Also, you should provide English-language translations of transcripts and recommendations.

The college will require verification that you have proper visa status to study in the United States. You probably will need to demonstrate that you can afford to pay for your education since financial aid opportunities for international students are highly limited.

TELL THEM MORE

To paraphrase the lyrics from the song "Summer Loving" in the musical and movie *Grease*, tell them more, tell them more, tell them more, more, more. There are times when the standard application, even with essays and recommendations, doesn't provide space for other essential—perhaps decisive—information to the admissions office.

When should you tell the admissions committee more? Often when you want to explain unusually low grades, whether in a key course or for a full semester or academic year. Perhaps you were sick, struggling with depression, working two jobs, raising young children by yourself, learning English, or caring for a dying parent. Perhaps you simply weren't mature enough yet for college.

Another far-from-rare situation is when there's an otherwise unexplained time gap when you weren't in school, at a job, or in the military. You may have been suffering from drug or alcohol abuse, dealing with physical or emotional illness, even been in jail. Don't pretend this type of black hole doesn't exist. Your application must be complete or it won't be processed, thus delaying or preventing acceptance. And it's better that you provide the adverse information rather than have the college discover it from another source.

Be frank and forthright.

Some transfer applications include an optional section to explain such situations—both what happened and why. For instance, the Washington University (Missouri) application extends this invitation: "If there are circumstances not reflected by your application responses or college record that you feel the Committee on Undergraduate Admissions should know, or if there are factors (positive or negative) that have affected your performance in college, please describe these." Similarly, the University at Albany (New York) application says, "If you wish you may describe any circumstances that have influenced (positively or negatively) your academic performance." And in an "additional information" section, the University of Dayton (Ohio) urges, "Please indicate any special circumstances you wish for the committee to take into consideration during the review of your application."

If the application doesn't ask, write a letter to the admissions office discussing the problems you had and how you handled them, and include it with your application and other supporting material.

The application material may invite optional, additional personal recommendations, providing another opportunity for you to tell the school more.

There are situations when you want to highlight a positive rather than explain or mitigate a negative. Let's say you've read in the press about an unusual program or faculty member at the target school. If that attraction doesn't fit naturally into the essay, you can include it in a separate note or cover letter explaining why you've chosen that college.

Or perhaps you've been in contact with a professor you hope to study or do research with. Again, point that out because it helps rationalize your interest in that school. At Williams College (Massachusetts), "sometimes a professor will go to bat" for a transfer applicant, notes associate admissions director Frances Lapidus.

TRANSCRIPTS

Generally, you'll need to provide official transcripts from every institution you've attended, even if you went there only for one course or a summer. Some colleges require two copies of each. The fee varies from college to college.

"The types of courses you have taken are as important as your grade point average," notes the University of Colorado at Boulder. So in addition to a transcript, some colleges want photocopies of the course descriptions of classes you've taken or are now taking from the catalogs of your present and former colleges. Those are used to help evaluate the content and difficulty of the classes and to help put the grade in perspective. They're also used to help assess transfer credits and the comparability of courses.

You may need an official high school transcript as well, particularly if you've completed fewer than a specified number of college credits. Some colleges demand a high school transcript from every transfer applicant.

International students: U.S. colleges understand that there are differences in how foreign colleges evaluate their students. Dartmouth College (New Hampshire) says, "The admissions office takes extra care in reading [applications] and evaluating students who attend non-U.S. schools. We recognize that each country has a particular way of evaluating their students. We measure your academic success by examining your academic record within your school's grading system. Experienced admissions officers are familiar with a variety of international grading systems." Similarly, Oberlin College (Ohio) says, "There is often concern that the admissions committee will not be aware of how rigorous a foreign

TO ORDER A TEST GRADE REPORT, CONTACT:

TOEFL Services
Educational Testing Service
P.O. Box 6151
Princeton NJ 08541-6151
(609) 771-7100

College Board SAT Program
P.O. Box 6200
Princeton NJ 08541-6200
(609) 771-7600

American College Testing Program (ACT)
P.O. Box 168
Iowa City IA 52243-1000
(319) 337-1000

school's grading system or national test scoring might be. Be assured that the international admissions staff is well informed about various national educational systems, and that we are well connected with Oberlin graduates from foreign countries who keep us informed about the special qualities of schools."

International students may need to submit a certified or notarized English translation of transcripts.

WRITING SAMPLE

Some colleges request a short writing sample, perhaps a two- to- five-page graded writing sample from a recent college course. At Sarah Lawrence College (New York), the sample must be a recent analytical or research paper, not a creative writing piece, and an instructor must have evaluated it. Wheelock College (Massachusetts) says an English composition, a history thesis, a literary critique, or a psychology report are among the kinds of writing samples that meet its requirement.

Even if a sample isn't requested, include one if you feel it will strengthen your application package. This optional sample may include the instructor's comments.

Pick an assignment that highlights your writing and analytical skills, even if you didn't get a perfect grade or even if the instructor made critical comments or suggestions.

OTHER INFORMATION

You may also be required to verify your health and your compliance with federal draft laws.

HEALTH INFORMATION

The college may require proof of vaccinations or good health.

On acceptance, you should be notified about the college's health insurance requirements, which the catalog or Web site may also describe. You may be told to buy coverage from a college-approved group program unless you present proof of your own or family coverage. International students may need proof of health insurance coverage from their home countries.

SELECTIVE SERVICE INFORMATION

The college may require proof that male applicants between eighteen and twenty-five are registered with the U.S. Selective Service System.

Think of the application as a package, not merely a form in which you fill in the blanks. There's a reason for each component in that package, whether it's mandatory (such as an essay, recommendation, or portfolio) or whether the college labels it as optional (such as a personal statement, interview, or writing sample). In planning, preparing, and submitting this package, your aim is to make it as easy as possible for a target college to say yes.

SOLVE THE
MYSTERIES
of
TRANSFERRING
CREDITS

FOR TRANSFER STUDENTS, ONE OF THE PRINCIPAL

concerns is how their credits will transfer. This is true whether you're transferring between four-year colleges, between two-year colleges, from a two-year college to a four-year one, or the other way around. That's why you should find out as soon as possible whether you'll lose any credits already earned and what impact that will have on your progress toward graduation. You may be able to get a preliminary estimate from a target school even before you formally apply, perhaps when you visit the campus with your transcript in hand, or if you bring your most recent transcript to a transfer fair at your current college.

CREDIT EVALUATION

Colleges evaluate transcripts and course descriptions in determining whether or not to count credits from other schools toward their own graduation requirements. The number of credits accepted determines class standing upon admission—freshman, sophomore, or junior status. (Most colleges don't grant senior status to incoming transfer students.)

Remember that the application requires you to disclose *all* institutions you've previously attended. Your work at another institution may have a bearing on your admissibility and acceptance, whether or not you expect to receive transfer credit for courses you took there.

If you have attended more than one institution so far, your target school may not review those credits on a piecemeal basis. As South Dakota School of Mines and Technology tells transfer applicants, "No transfer credit evaluation will be completed until ALL final college and university transcripts are on file." Its position on piecemeal credit evaluation mirrors that of most colleges.

The policy of the University of Saskatchewan, which is similar to that of many schools, indicates why and how transfer credits are evaluated: "The university accepts, for transfer of credit, courses from accredited institutions in Canada and elsewhere. Credit is awarded on a course-by-course basis for courses equivalent to those taught at the University of Saskatchewan. The purpose of evaluating transfer credit is to give students and applicants fair and reasonable credit for academic work which has been undertaken at another institution, and to reduce the likelihood of a student's having to repeat academic work in which he or she has already demonstrated competence."

Each college puts a cap on the number and type of transferable credits, and its policies may deter you from transferring or may influence your choice of a new college. The prospect of spending and paying for an extra semester or year may induce you to stay where you are. (The military academies don't accept any credits from other institutions, so even transfer students enter as freshmen.)

That may not be a concern if you're finishing an associate's degree at a community or junior college, especially if the school has a cooperative, reciprocal, or articulation arrangement with the college you're going to. But that policy can be significant if you want to transfer from one four-year institution to another or from a two-year institution to a four-year institution.

Transfer credits usually aren't included in your grade point average at the new school. Instead, you build a new GPA once you enroll. That may prove a blessing or a disappointment, depending on how well or poorly you've done so far. (*Note:* The transfer GPA *may* determine, however, your eligibility for a merit-based transfer scholarship.)

Unfortunately, you may get bad or incomplete information at your current school. The admissions staff at Fresno Pacific University (California) identify that as one of the most common mistakes for transfer students. Students "seek out counseling and advice from their current college counselors and get misinformation and adhere to it. For example, they take the wrong classes because they are advised to."

That's one reason why it's so important to explore transferability of credits early in the process to help avoid frustrations. Also, if you're applying in the fall to transfer the following fall, you can better tailor your spring classes at your current college to what's acceptable to your target college.

Even if credits do transfer, you need to determine *how* they'll be counted. Will those courses meet specific requirements at your new school, such as mandatory foreign language, writing, lab science, or math classes? Will they serve as prerequisites for upper-level courses in your major, minor, or any other department that interests you? A "no" answer may create a slowdown in your path toward a degree. At Randolph-Macon Woman's College (Virginia), for example, students from other four-year institutions can transfer up to seventy-five credit hours, but still must take at least half the credits for their major at Randolph-Macon. A growing number of colleges provide an online database that shows potential transfer students in advance how their credits may transfer. Some will provide a tentative evaluation of transfer credit shortly after they offer you admission.

Don't worry if your current school follows a term or quarter system while your target college is on a semester calendar, or the other way around. Colleges use formulas to calculate equivalencies under such circumstances. However, be sure to understand precisely how that formula is applied to your transcript to ensure receiving all the transfer credits you're entitled to. At Montana State University, "departments are prepared for substitution inquiries. Admissions determines equivalency of courses but departments may substitute transfer course work for degree requirements."

From the colleges' perspective, one concern is sequential courses to ensure that transfer students aren't underprepared because their prerequisites had different academic content. Here's another problem, as Champlain College (Vermont) explains: "Technical courses taken many years ago may have to be repeated because of substantial changes in the field." Red Rocks Community College (Colorado) warns would-be transfer students of its right to "validate and examine all credits to determine obsolescence of content. In the event that course work is found to be obsolete, you may be required to update the credit."

Colleges restrict the type of credits they accept or may specify a minimum grade in those courses. They may recognize only those courses that are comparable to their own or applicable to a degree program that they offer. For example, the University of Chicago (Illinois) counts only liberal arts courses worth at least three semester credits or four quarter credits, with a minimum grade of C or in some cases, B. The university doesn't take professional and technical credits in such areas as communication, speech, nursing, engineering, journalism, music performance, or business, nor will it count College Level Examination Program (CLEP) or correspondence courses. CLEP exams are an avenue to seek credit for what you've already learned through professional development, advanced high school classes, noncredit adult courses, or independent study. College policies vary on whether or not they accept CLEP results.

Common exclusions are "life experience" credits; correspondence classes; physical education; studies at unaccredited institutions; and college preparatory, vocational, and personal development courses. Don't hold high hopes about getting transfer credit for courses you took from the latest genre of unaccredited schools, online colleges. While several "virtual universities" have earned accreditation or are going through the lengthy procedures to earn it, others may be regarded as nothing more than high-tech diploma mills, often run on a for-profit basis. However, you shouldn't have a problem transferring credits from online courses that meet the other standards for acceptance if they're offered by traditional accredited colleges.

Remedial courses are usually excluded as well. They may have names such as Basic Language Skills, Spelling and Vocabulary, General Math Skills, Language Fundamentals, or Learning Success Strategies.

Transcript evaluations are done on an individual basis, and as the University of Kansas advises its transfer applicants, the fact a course appears on an approved list "is no guarantee that the course will transfer in your individual case."

In general, only undergraduate courses at an accredited institution are recognized. These are the principal regional accrediting agencies:

- Middle States Association of Colleges and Schools
- North Central Association of Colleges and Schools
- New England Association of Schools and Colleges
- Northwest Association of Schools and Colleges
- Southern Association of Colleges and Schools
- Western Association of Schools and Colleges

Institutions that belong to the Association of Universities and Colleges of Canada are considered accredited in that country.

North Georgia College and State University notes: "Even if the institution that the student last attended is an accredited institution, the director of admissions may reject all or any part of previously earned credits if there is any reason to believe that the quality of the educational programs of the previous institution is unsatisfactory."

Your new college may also recognize one of the specialized accreditation organizations such as the Accrediting Association of Bible Colleges, the Distance Education and Training Council, the Accrediting Council for Independent Colleges and Schools, the Association of Advanced Rabbinical and Talmudic Schools, and the Association of Theological Schools in the United States and Canada. However, that recognition usually applies only to regular academic courses at those institutions. Excluded courses may include ministry, pastoral studies, church education, and church administration, as well as courses designed to promote a particular denominational or doctrinal allegiance.

Some colleges count alternatives for students who've taken classes or enrolled at unaccredited schools. The University of Alaska at Fairbanks, for example, recognizes some national testing programs such as the College Level Examination Program, which is available for introductory courses. Another possibility is Credit for Prior Learning, which lets transfer students document learning that parallels specific courses on campus, subject to faculty approval. A third option is credit from military experience.

Colleges that recognize military educational credits can use an American Council on Education guide to make determinations. The University of Northern Iowa accepts credits "only for significant learning experiences that have nonmilitary applications. Basic military training is not eligible for credit." It also recognizes some credits from other military testing and educational programs.

And some schools provisionally accept credits from nonaccredited institutions. Ferris State University (Michigan) is among them, but requires you to maintain a GPA of at least 2.0 during your first year there. That means such transfer credits will count only if your academic performance at the new college meets specified standards. Auburn University (Alabama) also offers the option of provisional credits for students transferring from unaccredited institutions or programs.

Check into special transfer credit options. The University of Saskatchewan, for example, gives six credits to students who successfully complete a six-week summer session at Quebec University's full-time French immersion program.

If you've studied abroad, find out if those credits will count at your new college, whether they were earned directly from a foreign institution or under a program sponsored by a U.S. or Canadian college.

The maximum number of credits accepted can vary from program to program and major to major, even within the same university. And the review process can get quite specific. At Dalhousie University (Nova Scotia), all students must complete a "writing class," and transfer students who hope to have already met that requirement must show that at least 80 percent of their grade in a qualifying class was based on written work such as essays and reports, that there were frequent writing assignments to evaluate their skills, and that the class was small enough to allow individual advice and attention from professors or teaching assistants.

What if you're accepted to one program or major at a university as a transfer student, then switch to a program or major with different graduation requirements? If that happens, a reevaluation of transfer credits may be required. As Ryerson Polytechnic University (Ontario) says, "Transfer credits must be reevaluated if you change your program of study, as all programs have different course requirements for graduation. This does not apply from part-time to full-time or vice versa of the same program curriculum."

International students: While credits earned at non-U.S. and non-Canadian institutions may transfer, you may want to first have them assessed by a credential evaluation service. Your target school can provide a list of such services.

ARTICULATION AGREEMENTS

Articulation agreements—also known as "credit transfer agreements"—are contracts among two-year and four-year institutions, both private and public. They're designed to smooth the process of evaluating transfer credits. They also mean that if you continue in the same field of study, you should be able to complete your undergraduate degree on time, at least in most majors.

Incidentally, you may even get a leg up on acceptance when there is an articulation agreement in place. If you transfer with an associate's degree from a Florida community college, Florida Agricultural and Mechanical University will give "priority admission" over out-of-state applicants to programs that don't have limited access.

These agreements may be statewide or concentrate on community colleges within the four-year school's principal drawing area. As an example, the vice provost at Ohio State University at Columbus told the campus paper *The Lantern*, "We have articulation agreements with seven junior colleges in Ohio. We know exactly what their courses are worth, and we are making sure that students are doing work that will count for credit at Ohio State."

Each of the nine University of California campuses and twenty-two main California State University campuses determines its own general education and degree requirements. Each campus also works out articulation agreements with the state's 107 community colleges. Needless to say, that complex network of agreements can cause confusion and uncertainty when it comes to transfer credits.

That's why California developed an official statewide repository of transfer information called ASSIST—Articulation System Simulating Interinstitutional Student Transfer—to help applicants determine whether they'll receive credit for courses taken at a community college when they transfer to a four-year state institution. In addition, ASSIST shows how those courses apply to specific academic goals.

In New Jersey, Rutgers University maintains a similar Web-based data information system called Articulation System, or just ARTSYS. It helps prospective transfer students from all community colleges in the state to determine course equivalencies and whether courses meet general education requirements or requirements for majors at Rutgers.

Not all such agreements and arrangements are local or regional. For example, in 2001 the City College of San Francisco signed a national articulation and transfer network agreement with the more than one hundred historically black colleges and universities, most of them in the South and the East. The aim is to make such transfers easier. "It's a natural partnership," says George Boggs, the president of the American Association of Community Colleges, which represents more than 1,150 two-year institutions.

Lansing Community College (Michigan) negotiated articulation agreements with four historically black colleges, all in Georgia: Morehouse College, Spelman College, Morris Brown College, and Clark Atlanta University. Such arrangements can include special endeavors, such as its "Bridges" program with Spelman that provides better science-related opportunities for women who want to transfer there.

APPEALING CREDIT TRANSFER DECISIONS

You may be able to appeal an unfavorable transfer credit decision. To find out the proper procedure, contact the admissions office at your new college. The admissions staff may consult with the appropriate academic department for an opinion. You'll be expected to provide evidence to support the appeal, such as the syllabus and reading list from the course, information from the previous instructor, and copies of papers or projects you did in that course.

GETTING MORE TRANSFER FRIENDLY

In 1997, Texas directed public colleges in the state to improve their system for deciding how to apply community college credit. It did so because the state has no unified system of two-year colleges and because it's hard to coordinate their divergent course content and policies.

Elsewhere, you'll discover colleges becoming more flexible in recognizing transfer credits, especially in light of the heightened competition for transfer students. At Drury University (Missouri), the associate director of admissions and transfer coordinator, Chip Parker, says, "We have to be transfer friendly, especially if applicants have an associate's degree." For instance, an associate's degree is enough to fulfill most of Drury's core requirements. The college is also working to speed up the completion of so-called advance standing reports on what courses will transfer and how.

Colleges are making available comprehensive guides so you can assess which credits will transfer and what their equivalent courses are. Gonzaga University (Washington) uses its Web site to post its transfer guide for more than two dozen in-state and out-of-state two-year colleges.

With the growth of online courses and even degrees, executives of so-called "virtual universities" have signed an agreement to encourage transfer arrangements. "The intent of the accord is that students taking courses on-line will one day be able to transfer their course credits seamlessly from one virtual university to another," according to the *Chronicle of Higher Education*. "That would make it easier for students to earn degrees by weaving offerings from a number of on-line providers."

Here are other measures colleges are adopting to eliminate hassles and encourage transfers:

- Converting from terms or quarters to semesters. A shrinking minority of colleges—about 15 percent—still base their calendars on terms or quarters. That makes it tougher to calculate transfer credits and assess the comparability of courses. It also makes it harder for students to take courses at other consortium colleges that follow the more popular semester system.

- Earmarking more financial aid and recruitment funds for transfer students. That enables the college to spend more money to identify, recruit, and assist students who otherwise might not think seriously about transferring.

- Creating so-called "bridge" programs that work with community colleges to provide additional preparation and counseling for prospective transfers, especially for students hoping to switch to a more rigorous and competitive level of institution.

- Making it easier to transfer credits among institutions of higher learning within the state. That's particularly helpful where professional, job, or certification requirements have gotten stricter, meaning an associate's degree may no longer be sufficient for a career.

REPEATING COURSES

Should you ever voluntarily repeat a course, even if the credits are transferable and even if it meets a prerequisite or graduation requirement? Sometimes, yes. If you do so, ask whether the grade will be factored into the grade point average at your new college.

On the positive side and looking back candidly, you may realize that you didn't learn enough the first time through, or it didn't adequately prepare you for advanced or more rigorous courses that will follow at your new college, or it's been a long time since you took the class and you'd feel more comfortable brushing up.

On the negative side, it may keep you at college for an extra term or semester, may cost you additional tuition, and may prove boring. The British Columbia Council on Admissions and Transfer notes: "Repeating a course does not guarantee you a better grade. It takes a lot of self-control and discipline to do better in a course the second time around. Be prepared to put more effort into it than you did the first time."

Don't get lazy, let things slide, or think that you'll work things out sometime down the road. The stakes are high because each transfer credit you deserve but don't get will cost you time and money. All in all, there's a lot riding on the credit transfer process, including your ability to get into the courses you want when you want to enroll in them, the speed at which you'll finish your degree, and the total tuition you'll pay to earn it.

CREDIT EVALUATION POLICIES: A SAMPLER

"The college registrar, in consultation with the academic department chair-persons, evaluates transcripts to determine which credits will transfer to satisfy degree requirements. A preliminary evaluation of transfer credits will be mailed to you shortly after your admissions file is complete and you are officially accepted. Whenever possible, a final evaluation, which has been updated to include any recently completed course work, will be mailed before your enrollment."

—Randolph-Macon Woman's College (Virginia)

"As soon as your record has been assessed, the Registrar's Office will advise you, in writing, which credits have been awarded. The number of credits that have been approved, with their equivalencies, will be included in the letter. If more credits have been approved than can be applied to your program, you will be informed which credits have been selected. We will attempt to notify you as quickly as possible of allowable transfer cred-its. Before selecting classes, you should consult with the appropriate departments to determine how your transfer credits will fit into your aca-demic program."

—Dalhousie University (Nova Scotia)

TRADITIONAL FINANCIAL AID OPPORTUNITIES

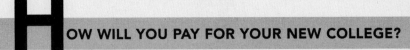

Remember that financial aid means not only scholarships and grants but also student loans, parent loans, and work-study programs.

Even if you don't qualify for financial aid at your current school, you might at another college. Why the difference? Lots of possible reasons. The new college may cost more. You may have depleted all your savings. You may have become financially emancipated from your parents. You may have given up a job to attend school full time. Your grades now may be high enough to qualify for merit-based scholarships. You may have made a sports team that has scholarship money available. You might fit into a special scholarship niche at the new college, such as those for children of alumni, children of employees, or residents of a particular town.

Filing deadlines vary among colleges, and some states set their own deadlines for state financial aid programs. Applying for admissions before the deadline may improve your chances of getting financial aid. Drake University (Iowa), for example, recommends that prospective transfers submit their applications and supporting documents ahead of the deadlines "to receive priority consideration for financial aid and scholarships."

Be forewarned: Some colleges give lower priority to transfer students than to incoming freshmen in their allocation of assistance. As Sarah Lawrence College (New York) tells prospective students, "The college's institutional aid budget for transfers is limited. Transfer applicants requiring financial assistance should discuss aid availability with the admission office early in the application process."

FREE APPLICATION FOR FEDERAL STUDENT AID (FAFSA)

If you've never applied for aid before, do so. Even if you were rejected before, try again. To do so, complete the U.S. Department of Education's Free Application for Federal Student Aid, familiarly known by its initials FAFSA.

The information is fed into a formula set by Congress to calculate your Expected Family Contribution, the amount you and your family are expected to

Cautionary words from the federal government: "Filling out the Free Application for Federal Student Aid and applying for student financial aid is free. You should be wary of mailings or Web sites that offer to submit your application for you, or to find you money for school if you pay them a fee. Some of them are legitimate, and some of them are scams. But generally any information or service you pay for can be had for free from your school or from the U.S. Department of Education."

—U.S. Department of Education

chip in. Colleges use the Expected Family Contribution to design a financial aid package based on the difference—if any—between your Expected Family Contribution and the cost of attendance, including living expenses.

Meet the deadline, and file as soon as possible after January 1 each year. Although you don't have to file your income tax return before submitting the FAFSA, filling out the IRS return first will make it easier to complete the FAFSA. If you use estimated income figures, you can use the Student Aid Report later to correct them after finishing your tax return. The Student Aid Report includes data from your FAFSA, as well as a calculation of how much assistance you may be entitled to under the federal formula. It also covers your financial aid history, including the amount of previous loans.

The award year for federal aid starts each fall. The Education Department processes FAFSAs from the January 1 before each award year begins until June 30 at the end of that award year. If you apply early in the application period, you have a cushion with enough time for your college to get the information and make any necessary corrections.

The same FAFSA form is often used for consideration by state financial aid programs, although their deadlines vary. However, your state or your new college may ask you to complete additional forms.

You can get the FAFSA form from your college or over the Internet at **www.fafsa.ed.gov**. About three million applicants are expected to use the site annually, according to the Education Department. You can use it not only to get forms but also to file them electronically. There's also a toll-free number (800-4FEDAID, or 800-433-3243) available seven days a week from 8 A.M. to midnight Eastern time. TTY users can call (800) 730-8913. By phoning, you can check whether your application has been processed, obtain a copy of your Student Aid Report, identify the current holder of your student loan, or ask questions about federal student assistance programs.

Warning: Be careful of nongovernment sites with similar domain names and Web addresses but operated by private companies that charge a fee for handling basic FAFSA forms.

COMPLETING THE FAFSA

Step One of the form seeks personal information, including name, address, phone, social security number, citizenship, marital status, and state of legal residency. Men ages eighteen to twenty-five must indicate if they're registered with Selective Service, a prerequisite to getting aid. Other questions include alien registration numbers for non-U.S. citizens, past drug convictions, and highest education level your parents reached.

This is a section where you mark which semesters or terms you'll be in school, and whether it will be full time, three-quarters time, half time or less than half time, as well as the degree or certificate you're working on. For undergrads, full time usually means at least twelve credits per term or semester; at least nine credits constitute three-quarters time; and at least six credits constitute half-time status.

Move on to *Step Two* to report your income and assets and those of your spouse. You'll be asked about the tax returns you filed, adjusted gross income, amount of income tax paid, exemptions, and earnings. FAFSA also requires the net worth of investments and businesses, the balances in your bank accounts, and the amount of veteran education benefits you anticipate receiving. Investments

COMMON ERRORS ON THE FREE APPLICATION FOR FEDERAL STUDENT AID (FAFSA)

- Using an invalid social security number
- Not signing the application
- Not providing a parent's signature when required
- Signing the application before January 1
- Attempting to file as independent when self-supporting status is not met
- Parent marital status is inconsistent with wages. If parents are divorced or separated, report only the custodial parent's share of income. If the custodial parent has remarried, you must report your stepparent's income as well.
- Reporting taxes withheld instead of taxes paid. Make sure you take the figure from the appropriate line on the tax return.
- Not reporting all untaxed income, including deferred compensation, Individual Retirement Account (IRA) and Keogh (another form of retirement account) payments, child support received, etc.
- Not reporting all assets. Do not leave these questions blank—enter 0 if the question does not apply.
- Not completing all sections of the application
- Assuming that aid can be transferred from one college to another

—Michigan State University Office of Financial Aid

exclude the home you live in, the value of prepaid tuition plans, and the value of life insurance and retirement plans.

Step Three covers questions about your children, other dependents, and veteran status.

Step Four requires detailed financial and personal information about your parents, such as their marital status, social security numbers, state of residency, tax returns filed, adjusted gross income, income tax, exemptions, earnings, bank account balances, as well as the net worth of their investments and businesses.

As you finish the form, list the colleges that will get your information and their codes. The codes are available at the Web site or from each college's financial aid office. If you plan to transfer in the middle of the academic year, list both your current college and your target schools.

Sign the FAFSA. So must one of your parents if you included their information.

The packet includes three worksheets. The first helps you calculate the answers to questions about earned income and child tax credits from the IRS, and welfare and social security benefits. The second covers child support received, tax-exempt interest, payments to tax-deferred pension and savings plans, housing and living allowances for the clergy and members of the military, and veterans' noneducational benefits. The third is for education tax credits, child support paid, work-study earnings, and some grants and scholarships.

Don't mail the worksheets. Keep them in case your college wants them.

You should get your Student Aid Report in the mail within four weeks after filing. If it's late, call the toll-free number (800-433-3243) or check online.

If you qualify for financial aid this way, it will be paid through your college. In most cases, the college first applies it to tuition, fees, and on-campus room and board. Any leftover aid will be paid to you to help cover expenses.

Be truthful. The federal government has the authority to verify the FAFSA information you provide, and there is a potential prison term and $10,000 fine for intentionally giving false or misleading information.

Be aware that if you have a drug-related conviction in your past, you *must* disclose it on your FAFSA. Depending on the nature, severity, and date of the conviction, a 1998 law may disqualify you from federal financial aid, at least temporarily.

VERIFICATION

Your FAFSA may be selected at random for a federally mandated quality control process known as verification. If yours is chosen, you'll have to submit additional information so the FAFSA and your tax returns can be compared.

SOME THINGS TO KNOW ABOUT QUALIFYING
FOR FINANCIAL AID

Be aware that your need for financial aid *may* count against you in the application process. Vassar College (New York) advises: "Vassar does offer need-based financial assistance to transfer applicants. However, due to the highly competitive nature of the applicant pool and the limited financial resources earmarked for transfer students, we are not need-blind in the evaluation of transfer candidates."

Tax data may not present an accurate picture of your ability or your family's ability to cover educational expenses. Here's advice from the U.S. Department of Education: "If you or your family has unusual circumstances (such as loss of employment) that might affect your need for student financial aid, submit this form, and then consult with the financial aid office at the college you plan to attend." Extenuating circumstances include loss of earnings because of natural disaster or disability, divorce or a parent's death after you filed the FAFSA, more than $3,000 in medical or dental expenses, lottery winnings, or capital gains from the sale of stocks or other investments.

Students frequently use the word "emancipated" to describe their independence from their parents and, thus, their claim that eligibility for financial assistance and the amount of aid shouldn't depend on their parents' income and savings. However, financial aid professionals avoid this term because a student who is considered emancipated by court order or by the Internal Revenue Service isn't automatically treated as independent for financial aid purposes. Instead, colleges may use a term such as "independent override" to describe their right to go beyond the federal criteria and exercise professional judgment on a case-by-case basis. It's left to the discretion of each college. Individual circumstances can range from a transfer student who quit a full-time job to attend college full time, unusually high medical bills that aren't covered by insurance, disinheritance because of a student's sexual orientation, or parents' death or divorce.

Your new college should have a procedure to review such situations. At the University of Mississippi, for instance, financial aid staff may exercise professional

QUALIFYING FOR INDEPENDENT STATUS

How do you qualify for independent status—meaning your parents' income and assets aren't considered in determining your eligibility for aid? You must meet at least one of six criteria to be treated as emancipated.

• Be at least 24 years old, or

• Be a military veteran, or

• Be an orphan or ward of the court, or

• Have legal dependents other than a spouse, or

• Be married at the time you file the FAFSA, or

• Attend graduate or professional school

judgment and change elements in the federal analysis to account for such unusual circumstances. Under its procedure, students must make a written request that focuses on events that affect their ability to pay college expenses and must provide supporting documentation, including a signed copy of their latest tax return. The university adds this caution: "Remember. Any adjustments made to your Student Aid Report as a result of your request for a professional judgment decision may delay or change your financial aid package."

The college may also offer assistance outside the normal financial aid channels to cover child-care costs. Ask.

FINANCIAL AID NOTIFICATION

When will you find out about a financial aid award? Usually when you get an admissions acceptance letter or soon afterward. At the University of Richmond (Virginia), "transfer students must complete the necessary applications for financial aid at the same time they apply for admission," says financial aid director Cynthia Bolger. "We then provide a decision regarding financial aid at the same time they are accepted by Admissions." Not all colleges follow the same pat-

tern, however. Be sure you are familiar with the pattern at the school to which you're applying.

If you plan to transfer for the spring semester, you may find financial aid tougher to get. That's because colleges generally allocate all their resources for the full academic year, starting with the fall semester. As Samuel Collie, the director of student financial aid at Portland State University (Oregon), explains, "If students are transferring mid-year, the new school may not have full funding left, and they may receive a less desirable financial aid package at the new school."

Some colleges, however, do reserve assistance for transfer students who arrive in the spring.

MAJOR CATEGORIES OF FINANCIAL AID

In most cases, a college will offer a financial aid package that may include a combination of subsidized and unsubsidized loans, scholarships, grants, and work-study jobs. Under each school's formula, the package is intended to make it mathematically possible for you to afford to attend, even if it would leave you in debt—perhaps significant debt—after graduation.

LOANS

The Federal Stafford Loan Program is at the top of the federal government's loan hierarchy. Under its Direct Loan Program, the federal government plays the dual roles of lender and guarantor, and distributes the funds directly to your college. Under the Federal Family Education Loan Program, loans are approved by commercial guarantors acting as federal agents, while commercial lending institutions such as banks provide the money.

There are three versions of loans available under both programs:

- Subsidized loans are for students who can demonstrate a need that is not covered by other aid. The government pays the interest while you are in school and during a grace period.
- Unsubsidized loans are for students who can't demonstrate financial need. You are responsible for interest from the time the money is paid, although

most students choose to have the interest capitalized, or added to the principal.

- Parent Loans for Undergraduate Students, known as PLUS, are for parents with dependent students and may be as much as the cost of education minus other financial aid. Parents do not need to demonstrate need to obtain a loan under PLUS. It's not government subsidized, so interest accrues from start through repayment.

In addition to direct loans, there is the Federal Perkins Loan Program for students who demonstrate financial need and are enrolled at least half time. The federal government subsidizes the interest while you're in college and during a grace period after you graduate or become enrolled less than half time. Interest can also be subsidized during a deferment period in situations such as unemployment and economic hardship.

Students should also be aware of two unrelated loan options in which colleges generally play little or no role, other than certifying that you're enrolled there and are eligible for assistance.

- The Federal Direct Consolidation Loan Program lets borrowers combine loans from different federal programs into a single loan with a single monthly payment.

- Private financial institutions also provide loans based on an analysis of your credit, your parents' credit, or both. Student aid professionals sometimes call these "alternative loans." The amount, interest rate, and repayment terms differ from institution to institution, and interest accrues immediately. You may need a credit-worthy cosigner. Most offer the opportunity to capitalize interest so you can wait until after graduation to start repayments.

Carefully compare each financial aid package with the cost of attendance, including travel and living expenses. Each college must manage its funds to best meet its own requirements and needs, and each has a different amount of money to allocate for aid from federal programs, endowments, and other sources. That's why financial aid packages with their mix of grants, scholarships, subsidized loans, unsubsidized loans, and work-study positions aren't like standardized

McDonald's meal deals. Even if the costs of attending two schools were identical—which is highly unlikely—it's highly unlikely that the aid package each offers you will be identical.

GRANTS

Unlike loans, there's no obligation to repay a grant, and they generally don't require anything beyond the FAFSA for application.

From the federal government: The federal government funds the Pell Grant program for students who are enrolled in a degree program and have financial need. There's also the federal Supplemental Educational Opportunity Grant for students with financial need.

From the state government: Some states have need-based grants for full-time students, part-time students, or both if they are legal residents of that state. Don't overlook these opportunities.

From the college: Your new college may have need-based grants funded by the school and by endowments. You don't need to repay these.

SCHOLARSHIPS

Like grants, scholarships are gifts, and thus there's no obligation to repay them. Many scholarships are based on academic achievement, areas of academic interest, business or union affiliations, state residency, or special talents such as athletics, the arts, or the sciences, with or without financial need. Some are awarded directly by the college or individual departments. Others require separate applications to the sponsors. Grants and scholarships from outside sources can affect the amount of assistance your college awards you.

There are a number of guidebooks and Web sites that list scholarships, as well as commercial services that charge a fee for trying to match you with suitable scholarship opportunities. Many financial aid professionals question the value of such commercial services, noting that the information is available without cost on the Web, at libraries, and through the colleges. A guidebook to scholarships may be a worthwhile investment, although much if not most of that information is available on the Internet.

WORK-STUDY PROGRAMS

Work-study jobs are available based on financial need. They generally involve on-campus jobs ranging from food service in the cafeteria to office work, research assistantships, and dormitory positions. Participating students must find qualifying jobs and work the hours to receive their paychecks, making work-study different from other aid programs, notes Rick Shipman, the director of financial aid at Michigan State University.

Your employer and the federal aid program each pay a percentage of the wages, and that percentage varies from college to college. Work-study income is taxable, and the college will send you a W-2 form and report your earnings to the IRS.

INTERNATIONAL STUDENTS

International transfer students are ineligible for U.S. federal aid, and many colleges don't provide them with scholarships or other financial assistance, with the possible exception of small emergency loans and small grants. That means you will have to demonstrate your ability to pay for tuition, fees, and other expenses to enroll by filing a Certificate of Financial Responsibility or similar forms. This statement by the College of the Holy Cross (Massachusetts) is typical: "Need-based financial aid is NOT available for non-U.S. citizens and non-permanent U.S. residents."

American University (District of Columbia) tells prospective international transfers that the federally funded programs it administers are available only to U.S. citizens and permanent residents. It suggests alternative places for international students to look, including embassies that might have scholarship funds or information about sources of funding. Your target college's financial aid office should be able to direct you to Web sites and to reference books such as *Funding for U.S. Study: A Guide for Foreign Nationals* from the Institute of International Education that covers scholarships, grants, fellowships, and paid internships.

If you're a U.S. citizen or resident who is transferring to a Canadian college, you'll probably be on your own financially as well. As Memorial University of

Newfoundland explains, "Each applicant would have to obtain his or her own financial assistance."

TAX BREAKS

The federal government and some states provide tax benefits for higher education expenses. If you qualify, these may make your new school more affordable.

Get the proper IRS and state tax forms and read the fine print, including the explanation of procedures, exceptions, and deadlines. This section provides an overview:

HOPE CREDIT

You may be eligible for a credit of up to $1,500 for qualified tuition, mandatory college fees, and related expenses. It's even available if you pay these expenses through a loan. There is a time limit: It's available only for your first two years of higher education and only for two years per student, so it's too late if you're transferring as a junior. You also must:

- Be enrolled at least half time for at least one semester, term, quarter, or summer school session during the year
- Be attending a public or private institution that is eligible for student aid programs administered by the U.S. Department of Education (Your new college will tell you whether it's eligible.)
- Be pursuing a degree or other recognized educational credential
- Have no felony drug convictions.

The Hope credit is gradually phased out if your modified adjusted gross income is $40,000 to $50,000 ($80,000 to $100,000 if filing jointly). It disappears if your gross income is at least $50,000 (or $100,000 filing jointly.)

The credit can't be more than the amount of tax you owe. If your federal income tax liability is only $750 this year, that's the maximum you can claim. Also, you're not entitled to claim the credit if your parents treat you as a dependent, but they can claim the credit.

LIFETIME LEARNING CREDIT

This one is worth up to $1,000 annually and is available for any higher education for an unlimited number of years. You don't need to be enrolled in a degree or certificate program as long as you're taking at least one course at an eligible institution.

You can't claim this credit if your modified adjusted gross income is at least $50,000 (or $100,000 filing jointly.) If your parents claim you as a dependent on their tax returns, they can take advantage of the credit but you can't.

Be forewarned: no double dipping. You generally can't claim more than one tax benefit for the same education expense.

STUDENT LOAN INTEREST DEDUCTION

The government allows a deduction of up to $2,500 on the interest you pay on student loans taken solely to cover qualified higher education expenses such as tuition, fees, room and board, books, and supplies. The amount of the deduction depends on your income and applies only to the first sixty months of repayment. You can't claim this deduction if you're listed as a dependent.

Understandably, finding the money to pay for college, living expenses, and personal obligations is a major concern for the vast majority of transfer students. And for those without deep personal or family pockets, financial aid from federal and state programs, your college, and private and civic organizations make it possible to attend school. That creates a big incentive to work to find every dollar of assistance you're legitimately entitled to.

FINANCIAL AID
OPPORTUNITIES
for
TRANSFER STUDENTS

BE ON THE LOOKOUT FOR FINANCIAL AID OPPOR-

tunities available only to transfer students. Think of them as incentives. Those based on merit without regard to financial need are designed to induce you to choose the school that offers them. Always ask admissions and financial aid officers at your target school about such opportunities. In addition, some colleges earmark a portion of scholarships and work-study jobs for transfer students. Ask about those too. (Information about financial aid for transfer students is frequently included with the admissions application, college transfer brochures, and on the college Web site.) Always meet the deadlines for scholarship applications. If you're finishing an associate's degree, discuss both merit-based and need-based scholarship programs with the transfer counselors at your present community college.

Also be aware that your prospective college may offer an early estimate service, as does Drake University (Iowa), to approximate each applicant's need-based financial aid eligibility.

TRANSFER STUDENT INCENTIVES: A SAMPLER

Here are some examples of special transfer student incentives from a variety of institutions. This is by no means a definitive list but is intended to provide a sampling of the types of opportunities available:

- Connecticut businesses and industries underwrite the need-based Etherington Community College Scholarship Program for students who transfer from community colleges in the state.
- The University of Texas at Arlington guarantees scholarships to financially needy students who graduate from certain Dallas-area high schools with at least a B average and then maintain a B average at any of the campuses in the Dallas County Community College District before they transfer.
- The transfer academic scholarship program at Texas Christian University is available to candidates with a minimum college GPA of 3.25 and at least twenty-seven hours of transferable course work. Those with the "very highest academic and personal credentials" compete for a full-tuition scholarship

covering up to sixteen credits per semester for up to four undergraduate semesters. Other scholarships in the program are worth up to $8,000 a year.

- Students who transfer to the State University of New York at Oswego with a grade point average of 3.3. or higher are offered a $1,000 merit award.

- Drury University (Missouri) awards academic honor scholarships of up to $4,000 to transfer students with at least thirty credits, based on their cumulative GPA. A GPA at your current college of 3.9 to 4.0 is worth $4,000; 3.6 to 3.8 is worth $3,000; 3.3 to 3.5 is worth $2,000; and 3.0 to 3.2 is worth $1,000. Transfers with fewer than thirty credit hours compete for academic honors scholarships of $500 to $2,500 based on their ACT scores, SAT scores, and high school GPAs, the same criteria as incoming freshmen.

- For transfers from two-year colleges that have articulation agreements with Hilbert College (New York), there are $2,500-a-year scholarships if they enroll full time in the same major as their associate's degree.

- At Bradley University (Illinois), there are $3,000–$5,000 transfer scholarships automatically awarded at the time of admission, and they're renewable if transfer students maintain at least a 3.0 GPA and full-time status. Other opportunities are available if they enroll part time.

- Southwest Missouri State University offers a $2,000 annual stipend for out-of-state transfers who arrive with a GPA of at least 3.25 and at least twenty-four transferable hours. It's intended to help offset the difference between in-state and out-of-state tuition. There's a similar program for transfers from Kansas, Michigan, Nebraska, and Minnesota. In addition, all mandatory out-of-state fees are waived for transfers who meet the same academic standards and if they have a parent or grandparent who graduated from the university.

- Drake University (Iowa) awards $7,500 achievement awards to outstanding community college transfers.

- At Auburn University (Alabama), there are three levels of merit-based transfer scholarships that depend on your prior GPA. The highest, which is valued at full in-state tuition, requires a minimum 3.7 GPA; the middle, worth

$1,000, calls for at least a 3.5; and the lowest is a $600 book scholarship for transfers with at least a 3.2 GPA.

• Similarly, Eastern College (Pennsylvania) pegs the size of its academic scholarships to your previous grades, using a sliding scale that ranges from $1,000 to $5,000 for GPAs of 2.0 up to 3.5-plus for full-time transfer students.

In some instances, scholarships are designed for transfers from specific colleges and for specific programs. For example, the University of Pittsburgh (Pennsylvania) offers Pitt Connection Transfer Scholarships to applicants to its liberal arts school from five designated community colleges.

There may be special applications for transfer student merit scholarships. That's the case at the University of Kentucky, which encourages transfers who arrive with at least sixty credits to compete for such awards. At the top end are renewable awards that cover in-state tuition, room and board, and a book allowance, plus a cash stipend. The university also gives a number of less lucrative merit-based scholarships. The application outlines the requirements and says, "Factors which are considered in the evaluation of scholarship applications include an essay, leadership experience, grades, extracurricular activities, work experience, awards and recognition, and community service." For the required essay of about five hundred words, students are asked to "describe the perfect day and explain what it tells about you as a person."

At Hood College (Maryland), transfers interested in a competitive Presidential Leadership Scholarship of up to $3,000 a year must demonstrate "not only a good educational background, but also evidence of commitment to a better world. That commitment may include family duties and responsibilities, or political, community, charitable and/or church volunteer activities." They must submit a letter of application describing "those services they believe worthy of such a scholarship and also describe their educational goals," as well as two reference letters attesting to their volunteer services.

Also at Hood, transfer contenders for the Hodson Scholarship for Academic Excellence must not only meet high academic standards but also must write two five-hundred-word essays on topics such as the elements of a successful college class, an instrumental educational experience, or a recent book. They undergo a faculty interview as well.

At some colleges, it's not necessary to separately apply for transfer scholarships. The State University of New York at Plattsburgh identifies eligible transfers during the admissions process and awards them one-time scholarships of $500 to $1,500, depending on their GPA, if they have graduated from a two-year school or are transferring as juniors.

PREPAID TUITION AND SAVINGS PLANS

Virtually all states now sponsor investment plans that use income tax incentives to encourage families to prepare early for the costs of college. These are known as "529" plans, a reference to the U.S. Internal Revenue Code provision that makes them possible. The details and procedures vary from state to state, but they fall into two basic categories: In a prepaid tuition program, the investment is intended to cover future tuition at a public institution. In a college savings program, the proceeds can be applied to future educational expenses at private or public institutions.

If you participate in such a program now, check with your present college, your target schools, and the appropriate state administrative agency on how to transfer the benefits. Arrangements tend to be easier if you're transferring from one public college to another within the same state, but all programs have procedures to address out-of-state transfers or transfers from public to private institutions. Although the rules vary from state to state, the program benefits may be lower if you transfer to an out-of-state college.

For more information on these programs, including a state-by-state breakdown, see **www.collegesavings.org** or **www.savingforcollege.com**.

RESERVE OFFICERS TRAINING CORPS (ROTC)

ROTC spans the boundaries among academic programs (because it carries academic credit), extracurricular activities (because it involves out-of-class time commitments), and financial aid (because ROTC scholarships are a major recruitment incentive). Those scholarships are based on merit rather than need. Depending on your college, they may cover the full cost of tuition (even out-of-state tuition if you attend a public college in another state), fees, and a book allowance while paying a monthly, tax-free stipend toward your living expenses.

Transfer students are welcome, whether or not they had participated in ROTC in their original school, and are eligible to compete for two-year and three-year scholarships. The air force also has a one-year program designed to meet its personnel need in certain fields.

Certainly there are noneconomic reasons why many students sign up for ROTC, including patriotism, a sense of duty, a commitment to public service, the guarantee of a well-paying job, a potentially secure and satisfying career after graduation, travel and adventure opportunities, preparation for business or political careers, and the prospect of the military paying for future professional and graduate training, including medical and law school. This book includes ROTC in the financial aid section because the economic aspects are a major draw and can influence your choice of college.

Would-be cadets and midshipmen must understand and accept that the government's primary motive, from the creation of ROTC in 1916 until the present, is to recruit, educate, and commission officers through campus-based programs.

At the same time, many colleges also regard ROTC as one means of recruiting highly motivated students. That's why many offer enrichment incentives to cadets, including transfer students, such as free room, free board, and supplemental scholarships. Some of those may be contingent on your choice of major and on maintaining a minimum GPA. In effect, the college incentive on top of the ROTC scholarship and stipend amounts to a free ride.

The army, navy, and air force each has an ROTC program, with some differences among them. The key similarities include a contractual relationship between participants and the U.S. Defense Department that require a set amount of military service after graduation. That obligation can be fulfilled in the regular armed forces, the reserves, or the National Guard. Those who complete the program and graduate from a four-year institution are commissioned as officers in that branch

ROTC WEB SITES

Army ROTC: www.armyrotc.com
Navy ROTC: www.cnet.navy.mil/nrotc
Air Force ROTC: www.afoats.af.mil/rotc.htm

of the armed forces. Navy ROTC midshipmen have the alternative option of a Marine Corps commission.

Army ROTC is the largest program, with units on about 270 campuses, followed by Air Force ROTC on more than 140 campuses in the United States and Puerto Rico, and Navy ROTC on about 70. If you're not transferring to a campus with its own ROTC unit, you may go to one that has a partnership, "cross-town affiliate," or consortium agreement with a unit at a nearby school.

If you have an ROTC scholarship at your current college, you can reapply for a scholarship and reenroll in ROTC at the school you're going to.

Cadets and midshipmen take military science courses that cover such topics as military history, tactics, leadership techniques, the law of war, weapons, military justice, personnel management, and communications. They also take part in physical fitness and field exercises, as well as other ROTC activities.

The normal four-year sequence includes courses in the freshman and sophomore years, but transfer students who miss those may be able to make up the work. For example, if you transfer as a first-semester sophomore, you can compress first-year and second-year classes on campus by taking those courses at the same time. "It's not a huge academic burden to catch up," says retired Lt. Col. Jim Rhoads, the scholarship and enrollment officer in the Department of Military Science at Michigan State University. Another alternative is to catch up through a summer program, with pay.

In most cases, you're expected to finish your bachelor's degree in four years but can apply for an extension of benefits for certain majors such as engineering where the normal academic program is longer. Scholarship requirements include U.S. citizenship, good grades, physical fitness, an approved academic major, and participation in extracurricular, leadership, athletic, or part-time employment activities. There are special incentives for military veterans returning to college and for students at historically black colleges, as well as special opportunities for nursing students.

The size of the scholarship varies according to the tuition at your college but is usually sufficient to pay the entire tuition bill at public institutions and a significant proportion, if not all, at private ones. Even without a scholarship, ROTC provides free books and supplies for its courses.

As you know by now, colleges value qualified transfer students, so many offer economic incentives to encourage you to choose them. To take the greatest advantage of these opportunities for transfer students, read all admissions and financial aid information carefully, paying particular attention to deadlines and requirements. If you're unsure about availability or eligibility, don't simply shrug off these questions but get the answers as soon as possible from the financial aid office.

13

GREAT NEWS—
YOU'RE
ACCEPTED!

CONGRATULATIONS! YOUR ACCEPTANCE LETTER

arrived in the mail.

In the movie *The Candidate*, Robert Redford plays an ambitious politician who runs for and unexpectedly wins a U.S. Senate seat. At the end of the film, bewildered and overwhelmed, Redford turns to an aide and asks, in essence, "What do I do now?" This chapter will help you answer the same question.

First, what kind of acceptance did you get? In most cases, it will be unconditional admission. Some colleges allow conditional admissions, depending on your prior courses and grade point average. In other words, they're willing to gamble that you can overcome past problems and succeed in a new setting. At Arkansas State University, transfer applicants with a cumulative grade point average below 2.0 may be admitted on academic warning if their GPA is at least 2.0 for the twelve most recent semester hours or if they've been out of college for a semester or longer.

Second, what if more than one college accepts you? You must decide quickly which offer to take. In part, you'll use the same considerations you weighed when choosing which schools to apply to. But now you've got more information, such as competing financial aid packages, promises of part-time employment, an understanding of which credits and how many of them will transfer, and perhaps the knowledge of where a friend may be transferring to.

Visit or revisit the campus. Call or e-mail a professor who teaches there in your prospective field of study. Call students from your hometown or region. Ask the admissions office for the names and phone numbers or e-mail addresses of recent alumni who live near you. If you're dissatisfied with the size of a college's aid offer or the mix of its components—scholarships, grants, loans, and work-study earnings—you may be able to negotiate a more attractive package with the financial aid office. This is particularly true if you can demonstrate unusual circumstances or if you can show that a competing school has made you a better offer. Check into the availability of part-time jobs and work-study opportunities.

Some colleges will reach out to you as well, offering to answer any lingering questions and to persuade you to enroll there.

Don't make a final decision until you've heard from all your target colleges. Even if there's an acceptance from your top choice, wait—one of the alternative schools may make an offer you can't refuse, such as an irresistible financial package, the promise of a starting spot on the basketball team, or the launch of a new major. As a student transferring from John Wood Community College (Illinois) put it, "Keep your options open. Don't choose the first one without weighing all the options."

RESIDENCY APPLICATION

If you're an out-of-state resident accepted by a public institution and want to be treated as an in-state resident for tuition purposes, you need approval of a residency application. Living in or moving to a state solely to attend school doesn't constitute legal residency, and a request to change your residency classification can be a time-consuming process.

This language is typical of what you'll encounter: "A person who has entered the state of Mississippi from another state and enters an educational institution is considered a nonresident. Even though he/she may have been legally adopted by a resident of Mississippi, or may have been a qualified voter or landowner, or may otherwise have sought to establish legal residence, such a person will be considered as being a nonresident if he/she has entered this state for the purpose of enrolling in an educational institution."

While the exact rules vary from state to state, in most cases, you must demonstrate that you've lived in the state for at least one year with the intent of staying there. The registrar's office can provide precise information on that state's residency requirements and on the process for proving compliance. Supporting documentation includes voter registration cards, driver's licenses, vehicle registrations, rent receipts, pay stubs or other documentation of earnings in the state, bank account records, and state income tax returns. West Virginia University cautions that a personal interview also may be necessary.

If you're fortunate, you live in a state or province with reciprocity arrangements and can pay discounted tuition. For example, as part of one such system called the Western Undergraduate Exchange, North Dakota State University charges residents of Alaska, Arizona, California, Colorado, Hawaii, Idaho, Manitoba, Montana, Nevada, New Mexico, Oregon, Saskatchewan, South Dakota, Utah, Washington, and Wyoming only 150 percent of the in-state rate, considerably less than other nonresidents pay.

Mississippi State University waives out-of-state tuition for transfers who arrive from a two-year college if they have completed at least fifty-four credits with a 3.5 GPA. They must maintain a 3.0 GPA to renew the full waiver, but can get a 50-percent waiver with a GPA of at least 2.5.

The New England Board of Higher Education runs a Regional Student Program that provides residents of the region with a tuition break—regardless of financial need—to study certain majors that aren't offered at public colleges in their own state. As an example, students from Connecticut, Massachusetts, and Vermont are eligible for the program if they study either chemistry and chemical oceanography, or physics and physical oceanography at the University of Rhode Island, while residents of Maine and New Hampshire qualify if they major in Latin American studies there. All seventy-eight public universities and colleges in New England participate. That lower tuition usually equals 150 percent of the college's in-state tuition.

FINAL TRANSCRIPT

Order a final official transcript from your current college, showing all work completed since the time of your application. This is important for evaluating the total number of eligible transfer credits, completion of prerequisites, and fulfillment of requirements at your new college. The application instructions will tell you where to have the transcript mailed.

COURSE REGISTRATION

Register for classes as soon as possible, especially if courses at your new college frequently fill or close out. You may be able to do this before orientation, or you may be required to meet or have a telephone conversation with your designated academic or faculty advisor before registering.

Either way, be smart about it. Review how the college evaluated your previous course work as prerequisites and equivalencies. Verify how many credits and specific required courses your major demands.

Use the catalog and course schedule—in print or online—as tools. Some classes are offered only in the fall or only in the spring. Some specialized courses may be offered only in alternate years. Pay attention to the course descriptions, which will list prerequisites. Some catalogs designate courses that meet graduation and distribution requirements. Find out who will teach the class, and call, write, or e-mail the instructor if you have questions about the content, level of difficulty, preparation, or workload. It's wiser to find out ahead of time rather than several weeks into the semester.

Feel free to contact academic departments, which can review your past work and recommend courses for your first term as a transfer student. Departments also may allow you to substitute transfer course work for degree requirements, but only if you ask with an explanation of your rationale.

Even if you're uncertain about all the courses you want that first semester, lock in as many as you can. Then use the drop-add period to round out and alter your schedule.

What if the computer tells you a class is already full? Here are several options: Some colleges reserve spots for transfer students. Some maintain computerized waiting lists. At others, instructors, professors, and department chairs have the power to lift the "official" ceiling on enrollment in their courses. Don't be afraid to ask them—after all, those courses are a principal reason, perhaps the principal reason, for your decision to transfer there. Another alternative is to ask your advisor to intervene so you can get in. Finally, if those measures don't work, follow my advice to students who want to take my closed-out courses: Attend each session during the first week or so in expectation that somebody will drop the course, and you'll then be ready to take his or her place when that happens.

Be on the safe side and earmark several alternate courses in case you still can't get into those at the top of your list.

VISIT CAMPUS

If you haven't visited campus yet, this is the time—especially if you've been accepted by more than one institution and haven't made a final commitment yet. If you did visit before, consider a return trip to refresh your memory and better help you prepare for the transition. Even if there will be a transfer student orientation program before the semester begins, an earlier visit can help head off difficulties.

Your key missions now are to:

- Familiarize yourself with campus. Where are the academic buildings, residence halls, athletic facilities, libraries, bookstore, and student union? If you plan to commute, where are the parking lots or mass transit stops?

- Make contact with academic advisors, professors, coaches, and organizational advisors. Discuss the classes you intend to take the next semester, the requirements for making a team, and time commitments for intercollegiate sports and extracurricular activities such as the campus newspaper, theater company, jazz band, or broadcast station.

- Check out housing options, on and off campus. Scout out nearby neighborhoods for comfort, lifestyle, and convenience. Look at classified ads and bulletin boards to find apartments and roommates. If you intend to live in a residence hall, you can identify your preferences.

- Apply for part-time jobs, on and off campus. See if the college has a job placement office. Read the help-wanted ads in campus and local newspapers. Bring copies of your résumé.

- Straighten out any unresolved issues concerning financial aid. You may be able to update the financial need information you provided when you applied and can inquire about work-study opportunities.

- Meet with an academic advisor or somebody in the registrar's office to discuss any disagreements, uncertainties, or discrepancies concerning transfer credits. If the new college didn't accept some courses, find out the reason. You may be able to change the advisor's mind by submitting more information about those courses, such as the syllabi, reading lists, papers or projects, and a letter from that instructor explaining details of the course.

• Introduce yourself to the chair or director of the program or department where you expect to major. As one transfer admissions expert recommends, "Start building relations early," because these people can become your advocates.

• Make sure as much of your past course work as possible will fulfill prerequisites for more advanced classes you intend to take. Again, you may be able to successfully plead your case with syllabi, reading lists, papers or projects, and information from former instructors. To manage your time efficiently, call, write, or e-mail in advance to set up appointments.

For more suggestions on what to look for on a visit and how to prepare, see chapter 6, "Make the Campus Visit."

PLAN YOUR COURSES WHERE YOU ARE

If you still have a full semester, summer, or both ahead at your present school, select courses that will benefit you the most at your new one. That includes classes that will meet its graduation, proficiency, general education, or prerequisite requirements. One goal is to do everything possible to finish your undergraduate degree on schedule.

Another reason to knowledgeably choose courses where you still attend is that courses may be oversubscribed or have waiting lists at your new school.

SIMULTANEOUS ENROLLMENT

You may have the opportunity to simultaneously enroll at both your current and future school for a semester or summer before your transfer officially takes effect, if they're in the same geographic area. As University of Missouri educational researcher Barbara Townsend observes, "Expediting degree completion by simultaneous enrollment makes sense from a student perspective." In one of her studies, 13 percent of transfers to a university continued to accumulate and transfer two-year college credits this way. (Incidentally, that's a variation on the more famil-iar practice of regular four-year students who take community or junior college classes simultaneously or during summers, often to fill prerequisites, save tuition dollars, or avoid overcrowded and closed-out introductory courses.) In most cases, however, you can only do this while you still have freshman or sophomore status.

Verify whether your new college requires prior approval for simultaneous enrollment and, if so, find out the procedure to request permission.

MONEY AND FINANCIAL AID

You need to plan a budget, realistically estimate what it will cost to be there, and determine where the money will come from.

Compare the financial aid package you're offered with the cost of attendance. Heather Andersen, assistant director of student financial planning at Drake University (Iowa), says, "Students don't always plan ahead to calculate how much money is needed to pay tuition and have enough for books and living expenses. Students who don't plan ahead usually do not borrow enough in the beginning and need to come back for a second loan."

Make arrangements to speak or meet with a financial aid counselor if you haven't already applied for aid. If you're dissatisfied with the college's offer, discuss it as soon as possible with the financial aid office. There may be a way to sweeten the pot, especially if you're a highly desirable transfer recruit and have offers from other colleges.

If you receive financial aid at your current institution, you need to take steps to avoid loose ends. That includes transferring your financial aid records to the new school. The University of Northern Iowa tells incoming transfers, "These records are necessary regardless of your previous enrollment load, period of enrollment, or financial aid eligibility at your previous college."

Here's what Slippery Rock University (Pennsylvania) tells students who are leaving for other colleges:

- Add the new college to your Student Aid Report or submit the report directly to the new school's financial aid office.

- If you now get a grant from a state agency, notify it of your enrollment change.
- Cancel any federal Stafford loans or disbursements that are already scheduled. Stafford loans can't be transferred, so you need to reapply for one.
- Provide deferment information to the lender or servicer of your current Perkins or Stafford loans once you enroll at your new school to avoid being asked to start repayments. Ask your new school to complete and submit the necessary deferment forms and to verify your enrollment.

DEPOSIT ON ACCEPTANCE

Usually you'll be asked for a pretuition payment, perhaps $200–$300, as a symbol of your commitment to attend. The money is applied toward your first semester's bill and may be refundable until a specified date.

MAKING PAYMENTS

Determine the college's payment options, including installment payments, due dates, interest rates, and late penalties. How often does the school send out bills? Can you use a credit card? Where do you send your payments? If a payment is late, will you be disenrolled from classes? What are your options if you run into monetary problems and can't make a payment on time?

Always check your bills carefully, even if they're paid through your loan or grant. First, the bills should accurately reflect the amount and nature of your financial aid. If they don't, make sure the error is corrected promptly.

If you transfer to a college that charges tuition by the credit hour rather than a flat amount per semester or term, be sure the statement accurately reflects the number of credits you're taking. If there's a difference in the housing fee based on the dorm you're assigned to or based on whether you live in a single room, a double, a suite, or an on-campus apartment, be sure the bill shows the correct category. If there are several meal plan choices, be sure you're charged for the right one. Other potential mistakes to look out for: charging out-of-state tuition if you've established in-state residency or have a waiver; parking fees if you don't have a vehicle at school; and mandatory health insurance fees if you're covered by a family or personal policy.

INTERNATIONAL STUDENTS

Once you're accepted, it's time to start moving on visa and immigration requirements.

If a spouse, children, or partner will accompany you, find out how to meet their legal, immigration, insurance, housing, and employment requirements. Among the questions needing answers are these: What types of jobs are your spouse or partner allowed to hold, and is there heavy competition for those jobs? What income tax liability will they face? What arrangements can be made for child care or schooling for your children, and is there a fee for those services? Will your health insurance plan cover them and, if not, what alternatives are available? If you're bringing a vehicle with you, must you reregister and insure your vehicle in the country where you will attend school?

Find out the location of your own country's embassy or consulate closest to your new college.

International students coming to the United States need a certificate of eligibility, technically called the I-20 form, and must present it to a U.S. embassy or consulate to receive their F-1 student visa. You can get a new visa only from an embassy or consulate outside the United States, and embassies may differ on their visa application procedures. Many, including those in Canada and Mexico, require an appointment, which will be conducted in English, to process student visas. You need documents to demonstrate that you intend to return to your home country after college, such as family ties, real estate, investments, or a job there.

NAFSA, the Association of International Educators, cautions, "If you are not able to articulate the reasons you will study in a particular program in the United States, you may not succeed in convincing the consular officer that you are indeed planning to study, rather than to immigrate. You should also be able to explain how studying in the United States relates to your future professional career *in your home country*." During your interview at the consulate or embassy, you're expected to speak on your own behalf, in English, and may be asked to explain how the planned academic program fits your career plans. You may also be asked about dependents who will remain behind in your home country and about any employment plans in the United States. Be candid and concise, and maintain a positive attitude.

The association also advises:

Applicants from countries suffering economic problems or from countries where many students have remained in the United States as immigrants will have more difficulty getting visas. Statistically, applicants from those countries are more likely to be asked about job opportunities at home after their study in the United States. Your main purpose of coming to the United States should be to study, not for the chance to work before or after graduation. While many students do work off-campus during their studies, such employment is incidental to their main purpose of completing their U.S. education. If your spouse and children are remaining behind in your country, be prepared to address how they will support themselves in your absence. This can be an especially tricky area if you are the primary source of income for your family.

It is essential that you don't withdraw from your present college until you receive a definite notice of acceptance, including visa.

U.S. CITIZENS TRANSFERRING TO CANADIAN COLLEGES

U.S. citizens transferring to Canadian colleges must apply for student authorization—also called a student visa. "You'll need to present your offer of admission from the college, an up-to-date passport, proof of sufficient funds or a reliable source of money to cover tuition and living expenses, medical clearance, and an application processing fee. When you arrive in Canada, you may be asked for a list of items being shipped separately. All international students, regardless of the country they are from, are subject to the same conditions," notes Queen's University (Ontario).

U.S. citizens are eligible to apply for their student authorization at the port of entry, but the Canadian Bureau for International Education recommends doing so in advance to save time. You can apply through the nearest Canadian consulate. Please note: If a medical exam is required, Citizen and Immigration Canada accepts exam results only from designated medical practitioners, including ones in the United States. Your college or the bureau can assist you in locating one.

Immigration officers also may ask for proof that you can pay for health insurance. Most Canadian colleges have insurance plans for international students.

In addition to the national requirements, the province may add its own. For example, McGill University (Quebec) tells applicants who are not citizens or permanent residents of Canada that they need student authorizations from both Canada and the province of Quebec.

HOUSING

Where do you plan to live? On campus or off? In a traditional dorm, a co-op, a fraternity or sorority, a house, a program-based facility, or an apartment?

That may not be a serious issue if your new college requires all undergrads to live on campus, or at least unmarried undergrads or undergrads below a specified age. That also may not be an issue if your current and future colleges are in the same community or if you intend to stay with your parents. But most transfer students need to make new living arrangements.

Considerations include your budget, proximity to campus, available parking, public transportation, access to shopping, and neighborhood safety. If you have a spouse, partner, or children, that can affect where you want to live and possibly how much it will cost to live there.

Is special housing available for transfer students? Cornell University (New York) has what it calls the Transfer Center, a residential program house for about two hundred transfer students and their resident advisors, who are former transfer students themselves. "Whether you live in the building or not, all transfer students are welcome to join. The program supports activities and social events for transfer students and offers support and information aimed at helping all transfers make a smooth transition to the university."

Your new college is the starting place for housing information, even if you've chosen an all-commuter school. Some colleges assist new students with housing placement and matching, even off campus, but all have information about what's available in the community.

If your new college offers on-campus housing, you'll get a housing application either with your acceptance letter or soon afterward. Supplement that material with information on the housing service's Web site. Increasingly, dorms have computer labs, ATMs, convenience stores, free basic cable and local telephone service, laundry rooms, recreational facilities, tutoring programs, and study lounges. At many colleges, housing facilities are co-ed, with men and women in adjacent rooms, on separate floors, or in separate wings, although there may be all-male or all-female options. At other campuses, all housing is either all men or all women. Some colleges ban smoking in all dorms.

Costs may be more predictable, too, if you live on campus.

Don't procrastinate. Demand for on-campus housing may exceed supply, and current students may get preference. Some colleges guarantee housing for every transfer student, but others don't.

Submit your on-campus housing application as soon as possible to ensure the widest choice of accommodations, especially if you have a preference such as a single room, a nonsmoking dorm, a "quiet" floor, an apartment, or a theme-based dorm. Family housing may be limited too. If you have a specific roommate in mind, make that clear when you apply for housing. If you prefer another transfer student in your room or suite, specify that.

Like many colleges, Arkansas State University asks prospective on-campus residents a number of personal questions to help make appropriate housing assignments. Among them are choices about smoking, alcohol use, majors, music preferences, language, special needs, and plans to remain or leave campus on most weekends. Here are several others: "Am I a morning or night person?" "I prefer to study alone or with others," and "I feel most comfortable in my room when: it is neat and everything is where it belongs; it is fairly neat and everything is usually put away; it is clean, but sometimes gets pretty cluttered; it doesn't really matter what it looks like as long as it is relatively neat." Another issue to consider: "When I study, I: require absolute quiet and am easily distracted; like a low background noise or music; am able to tune out most noise and am not easily distracted."

Wherever you opt to live—off campus or on—you'll be expected to put down a deposit toward your rent. Utility companies—phone, electric, gas, and cable TV—may demand security deposits as well if you haven't established a credit record with them.

Start thinking about what you'll need for your new accommodations. Some on-campus residential facilities already have mini-refrigerators, for example, but you may want to bring or buy a microwave, a toaster-oven, an electric coffeemaker, a stereo, a television, and a VCR or DVD player. It would be wise to check on what appliances can be brought in. Not all schools allow everything. If you're moving into an apartment, you'll need furniture, cooking gear, dishes and silverware, sheets and towels, and other basics.

If you've never lived with anybody except your family before, get ready for some life lessons in compromise, peer pressure, and privacy. If you'll have a room-mate, apartmentmate, housemate, or suitemate, get in touch as soon as you know who he or she is. That way you can divide responsibility for arranging utilities and can decide who will bring what furniture and appliances. If your new apartment has only one allocated parking space but the tenants have more than one vehicle, decide how to handle that. Do you want a second phone line for Internet access? Do you want to pay for cable TV or a cable Internet connection?

Do you plan to eat some meals together? If so, who will shop, who will cook, who will wash dishes, and how will you assess the expenses? You also need to agree on ground rules such as cleaning duties, cleaning schedules, noise levels, and overnight visitor policies.

If you intend to live in a residence hall, find out your meal-plan choices. Some colleges require dorm students to sign up for a cafeteria plan, although you may have options about the number of meals you buy each week.

TRANSFER STUDENTS' RIGHTS AND RESPONSIBILITIES

WHEN YOU ARE OFFERED ADMISSION

You have the right to receive an official notification of acceptance and at least one month prior to enrollment:

- Written evaluation of courses and credits accepted for transfer credit and their course equivalencies;
- An outline of transfer courses and requirements which these courses and requirements will satisfy for the degree you are seeking;
- A statement about your previous grade-point average/quality points and how they will affect or not affect your new index;
- A written analysis of the number of semester/quarter-hours and credits required to complete a degree in your currently stated major field of study, if applicable.

You have the right to wait to respond to an offer of admission and/or financial aid until May 1. It is understood that May 1 will be the postmark date. Colleges that request commitments to offers of admission and/or financial assistance and housing prior to May 1 must clearly offer you the opportunity to request in writing an extension until May 1. They must grant you this extension, and your request may not jeopardize your status for admission and/or financial aid.

AFTER YOU RECEIVE YOUR ADMISSION DECISIONS

You must notify each college or university that accepts you whether you are accepting or rejecting its offer. You should make these notifications as soon as you have made a final decision as to the college you wish to attend.

You may confirm your intention to enroll and, if required, submit a deposit to only one college or university. The exception arises if you are placed on a wait list by a college or university and are later admitted to that institution. You may accept the offer and send a deposit. However, you must immediately notify a college or university to which you previously indicated your intention to enroll.

Although you'll feel euphoria and pride at your accomplishment, the acceptance letter is no justification for resting on your well-deserved laurels. There's a lot more planning and labor required between the moment you open the envelope and the first day of classes, which may be months away. Follow the college's requirements as outlined in its acceptance letter and accompanying material, as well as any other requirements that are explained in later correspondence. Anything you overlook or ignore during this period may be difficult to rectify once classes begin.

IF YOU ARE PLACED ON A WAIT LIST OR ALTERNATE LIST

The letter that notifies you of that placement should provide a history that describes the number of students on the wait list, the number offered admission, and the availability of financial aid and housing.

Colleges may require neither a deposit nor a written commitment as a condition of remaining on a wait list.

Colleges are expected to notify you of the resolution of your wait list status by August 1 at the latest.

—National Association for College Admission Counseling

If you have dietary restrictions, ask how the campus dining service can accommodate you. You may have medical limitations and need a low-fat, low-sugar, or low-sodium diet. You may be Jewish or Muslim and have religious constraints on what you eat. Or you may have philosophical preferences such as vegetarian or vegan. If the college can't suitably meet those dietary needs, ask about an exemption from the meal-plan requirement.

MEDICAL FORMS AND INSURANCE

The college may mail you a mandatory health examination form. It may include immunization information required by state law. Also, ask your personal physician whether you should bring copies of any medical records with you.

Follow the college's requirements for medical insurance. If you have the option of obtaining your own insurance, make arrangements as soon as possible. Ask your current insurer whether your policy will cover you in a new location. If you've been insured through your employer's group policy and want to retain that coverage, check on the procedures and premiums for converting to COBRA coverage.

14

MAKE THE MOST
of the
ORIENTATION
PROCESS

CHANGE, NO MATTER HOW WELCOME, IS DIFFICULT

for everybody, and unexpected snags and snafus can arise no matter where you go. An effective orientation process—even if it lasts only part of one day—can help you adjust to your new living and learning environment. It's your first chance to meet other newcomers in the same situation and to talk with former transfers who've successfully gone through the process and can offer firsthand suggestions about what to do and what not to do.

Orientation can cover everything from familiarizing transfer students with the campus and its services, facilities, and academic and behavioral expectations, to the availability of medical care, security, and use of the college's e-mail system. During orientation, you may be able to take placement tests to opt out of required courses or prerequisites, generally in English, science, math, or languages.

Whether you'll be a commuter, live on campus, or live off campus, it's important to participate.

"Don't assume that you don't need an orientation just because you've already been in college," says Richard Adle, the assistant vice president for student life at Hilbert College (New York). Janet Felker, a transfer advisor at Salt Lake Community College (Utah), agrees: "Attend orientation, and make an appointment with your advisor before registering." Texas Woman's University says failing to attend orientation is one of the most common mistakes that transfer students make.

Attend even if you intend to be a part-time student. The information will be just as valuable as for full-time transfers.

Often you'll see significant differences between the transfer student and freshman orientation processes. For one, transfer orientation tends to be shorter, principally based on the assumption that transfer students are more mature, more self-directed, and better able to figure things out for themselves. Some colleges provide special orientation materials for transfers, while others don't. Either way, the goal is to speed your integration with the college. "In general, we try hard to make transfers feel like regular students as quickly as possible," says Wake Forest University (North Carolina).

Northern Arizona University runs one-day orientation sessions for transfers and two-day sessions for freshmen. "However, transfers are allowed and sometimes even encouraged to attend our two-day sessions, especially for the transfer who has a majority of transfer hours from College Level Examination Program testing or has lived at home and attended community college. They may benefit from the comprehensive two-day orientation," coordinator Cynthia Hernandez says.

For multiday orientations, find out if on-campus housing and meals are available, either for a fee or without charge. Alternatively, the college may reserve rooms at local motels at discounted rates.

You may have a choice of when to attend. If you plan to transfer for the fall, the new college may allow you to attend summer orientation—which is often less chaotic and less crowded—or right before classes begin in the fall.

Prepare *before* orientation. Read or reread all the literature sent to you and check or recheck the college Web site and catalog. Those steps will make you more familiar with the college and can answer many questions that inevitably will be on your mind.

Once you arrive, get to know the campus. Walk around. Find the buildings where your classes will take place. See how the libraries operate—hours, reserve books, periodical and journal collections, small group study facilities, circulation policies, and computer stations. Check out the services available at the student union or student center. Scout out places to eat lunch or snacks. If you haven't formally toured the campus on a previous visit, do so during orientation.

WHAT ORIENTATION SHOULD COVER

Here are some topics that transfer orientation *should* cover. If yours doesn't address some of them, the responsibility to find out about these topics falls on your shoulders.

ACADEMIC ADVISING, REGISTRATION, AND PLACEMENT TESTING

What's the process for registering for classes? Who are your advisors and how do you arrange to meet with them? What tests are available to place out of required classes or meet graduation requirements, such as foreign languages, writing, speech, or math? How can you meet with individual faculty members to discuss the content of their courses and their suitability, based on your background and interests? Before arriving at orientation, find out whether your new school will preregister you for required courses.

At some colleges, there may be a single advisor assigned to all students within one or more majors, leaving it up to you to seek additional guidance from a professor. In contrast, all arriving transfer students at Marlboro College (Vermont) are assigned both a peer advisor and a faculty advisor. That college is small enough that its director of advising can assess students individually to determine the most suitable professor for each.

ACADEMIC WORKLOAD

Discuss the recommended course load for transfer students, including the number of actual hours you're expected to spend each week in classrooms and labs and the typical amount of out-of-class study time. This will fluctuate from major to major and depends in part on your own study habits and techniques. Get at least rough guidelines to help you estimate how much time will be available for a job or extracurricular activities. Some transfer students find it advantageous and less stressful to take a reduced credit load during their first semester, especially if that won't affect their financial aid or slow their progress toward graduation.

ATHLETIC OPPORTUNITIES—INTERCOLLEGIATE AND INTRAMURAL

What teams or clubs are there, and how can you get involved? The athletic director may make a presentation during orientation, and you may be able to set up a one-on-one meeting with a coach if you haven't done so before. If your transfer orientation takes place in late summer, athletes in fall sports may already be on campus, so you can watch them practice and chat with a couple of them.

ON-CAMPUS ORGANIZATIONS

There may be presentations, booths, and information tables on behalf of campus groups. They'll include organizations that deal with performing arts, media and press, fraternities and sororities, ethnicity, religion, intramural sports, student government, international issues, recreation and travel, politics, community service, and public affairs. You can speak individually with their representatives about meetings, programs, and other ways to become involved. Your orientation packet may include information and contacts for these groups.

At some colleges, organizations receive a list of arriving transfer students and may send you information in advance.

CODES OF CONDUCT, ACADEMIC INTEGRITY REGULATIONS, AND THE CAMPUS DISCIPLINARY PROCESS

What are the college's expectations for personal conduct? What are the rules on alcohol and drug use? Beyond the disciplinary system, what resources are available to help overcome substance abuse? Is there a formal honor code that you must sign, and what does it cover? Is there a faith-based set of behavioral expectations?

What is the college's code on ethical use of computers? A comprehensive code will address a range of topics, including hacking, unauthorized copying of licensed software, privacy, harassment, pornography, links, misrepresentation, and use of individual, course, and departmental Web sites.

Is there an ombuds office to help resolve problems, conduct impartial inquiries, and cut through red tape when the ordinary academic and administrative channels don't work, or when you feel uncomfortable using them? If so, where is the office and how do you use its services?

You need to know how to file a complaint if, for example, you're subjected to sexual, ethnic, or other harassment, if you suspect another student is cheating, or if you believe a faculty member is treating you in an unfair or discriminatory way.

OPPORTUNITIES FOR ON-CAMPUS AND OFF-CAMPUS EMPLOYMENT

If your new college has a job placement center, there may be a presentation about its services. At Fresno Pacific University (California), for instance, "We hold student employment workshops during orientation and include Career Resource Center information in our packets," says Don Sparks, the assistant dean of student development programs.

In job hunting, don't rely solely on the hourly rate. Here are other important considerations:

- *Proximity and transportation:* How close is the job to where you live and to campus? How will you get there? Will you need to pay for mass transit or parking?
- *Schedule:* Is the employer flexible enough to work around your class and study schedule? Will the employer accommodate college holidays and vacations? If you work nights and weekends, does public transportation run those days and hours?
- *Benefits:* If you work enough hours, are you eligible for paid vacation, health insurance coverage, and sick time?
- *Getting paid:* To help you plan and stick to a budget, will you be paid weekly, every two weeks, or monthly?
- *FICA (social security taxes):* Working for the college may save you the FICA tax, thus adding to the amount of money you take home.
- *Experience:* Does the job relate to your major or career plans? Will it develop or improve marketable skills? Are there opportunities to move up into supervisory or managerial positions?

International students need to verify what types of employment are allowed and what ones are off-limits. For example, international students transferring to Canadian colleges may be authorized to work only on campus.

Other job-related considerations to check during orientation include the impact of your outside earnings on financial aid eligibility, any restrictions on the maximum number of hours full-time students are allowed to work, and whether the college will let certain paid work fulfill internship requirements in your major.

PAYING FOR COLLEGE

Confirm your financial aid status and package, including loans and scholarships. If you haven't done so already, make payment arrangements for tuition, fees, and housing bills. Depending on the college, you may be able to pay in installments or to charge these expenses to your credit card, giving you a small time cushion.

If you envision financial problems right away, now is the time to discuss and try to resolve them. Financial aid advisors may participate in orientation sessions too, giving a general presentation, staffing information tables, or both. At Michigan State University, financial aid officers are at the orientation site with computers to immediately access transfer students' files and make any needed changes in their financial aid packages.

HOUSING

If you haven't finalized housing arrangements yet, do it now. Stop by the campus residence halls or apartments—you may find anything from high-rises to town-houses to Gothic-style buildings to restored Victorian-era mansions. Look at classified ads for off-campus housing. Check bulletin boards in the student union, campus center, or housing office for people in search of roommates, apartment-mates, and housemates. Post your own notice. Visit nearby apartment complexes.

As you look around, keep in mind parking, transportation, safety, rent and utility costs, comfort, quality of the accommodations, and the neighborhood.

SECURITY

These issues include access to buildings—a growing number of institutions use electronic swipe cards to control entry to dorms, academic buildings, and other facilities. Find out about late-night escort services, the emergency call box system, and parking lot security.

HEALTH

You need to know about medical services and health care, including the location of an on-campus clinic if your new college has one. Key questions include: What medical, dental, psychological, vision, and pharmacy services are offered? What are the clinic's operating hours? How do you make appointments? Who is eligible for care, and can spouses, partners, and dependent children use the services? Can you discuss health concerns over the phone with a nurse, physician, or other medical professional? Are there health education programs and support groups on campus?

Ask about fees for services, including office visits, X rays, and lab tests. Ask what is covered by medical insurance, and how you pay for anything that isn't covered. Ask about treatment for chronic health problems. Ask if there's information on family planning, birth control, and prevention of sexually transmitted diseases.

Ask about arrangements if you need regular allergy shots, need to dispose of insulin syringes, need to fill prescriptions from home, or need immunizations.

INTERNATIONAL STUDENT ORIENTATION

Transferring to a Canadian college from one in the United States? Or from a Canadian college to one in the United States? If so, attend any extra orientation session for international students. You'll need the latest information about immigration, visas, insurance requirements, taxes, and employment regulations. If there's an international center, drop by and become familiar with its services.

MORE THINGS TO DO

Orientation is also the time to take care of a lot of routine paperwork and errands, such as obtaining your student ID card, getting a parking permit, buying a bus pass, making extra copies of keys, and for international students, double-checking visa status.

Set up a checking account at a local bank or credit union now—it will be less hectic than during the start of the semester. Even if merchants accept checks from your hometown bank, you may want to switch to a local financial institution for convenience and to avoid ATM fees.

If you've moved to a different state, will you need to change your motor vehicle registration, driver's license, and insurance company? Not necessarily, if you maintain your full-time student status, but it may be cheaper to do so. Talk with your own insurance agent and call a couple in your new community, perhaps one who is affiliated with the same insurance company you've been using.

If you're a resident of another state who is transferring to a public college, you may plan to work full-time and attend classes part-time for the first year to qualify for lower in-state tuition. If so, you'll need to show an intent to become a legal resident of your new state—and the college will demand documentation. Depending on the state's requirement, that may mean switching your car license and registration, registering to vote there, and paying income taxes in your new state. Ask the admissions or registrar's office about the requirements and procedures, and take care of the paperwork right away.

RELIGION AND FAITH

If you want to find a place to worship or pursue faith-based activities, many denominations and nondenominational groups have campus facilities and some sponsor registered student organizations. Others have churches, synagogues, mosques, and sanctuaries located close to campus. During orientation and the first weeks of classes, try to visit more than one house of worship in the community to see where you feel most comfortable.

While an off-campus institution may be less convenient, it also may provide contacts in the community and a chance to meet people unaffiliated with the college. Many provide free transportation from campus to worship services and other activities. In addition to formal events, you may be invited to share meals or holidays with local families.

OPTIONAL ACTIVITIES

Orientation needn't be all work and no play. The college may put on social events as well, including informal receptions where you can mix with other transfer students along with faculty and staff. During University of Montana orientation sessions, students can take advantage of the college's proximity to the outdoors by joining guided whitewater raft trips and day hikes for a fee.

Some colleges host orientation activities for parents, spouses, and guardians. They take place separately from student orientation but at the same times, and they address issues that face the students. At the University of Montana, those sessions cover academic expectations and advising, residence halls and campus life, security and health services, and social activities and career services. Housing and meals for family members may be available.

Don't treat orientation as a burden or a bore. Instead, regard it is as time well spent in preparing for a new academic environment and in relieving lingering doubts or uncertainties about switching colleges. No matter how much you already know about the school, you'll learn more useful information during orientation, making it easier to concentrate on studies and extracurricular activities once the semester or term begins.

SELF-ASSESSMENT OF PAST AND FUTURE

You're in a new setting, among new people, and facing new challenges and opportunities. Use orientation as a suitable time to reassess your past and your future. At Central Michigan University's transfer orientation, students receive this checklist:

WHERE I'VE BEEN (MARK THE AREAS THAT ARE TRUE FOR YOU.)

- Low high school GPA
- Lower GPA than desired at previous college
- Lack of motivation to study
- Difficulty managing time
- Difficulty managing work, family, child care
- Hesitant to ask for help when needed
- Personal issues
- Financial struggles
- Unsure of major and career options.

WHERE I'M GOING (MARK THE AREAS THAT WILL BE YOUR GOALS.)

- Schedule time to study and complete assignments. Stick to it!
- Visit my instructors during office hours.
- Get free tutors for courses.
- Meet with my academic advisor to review requirements.
- Get involved!
- Utilize the Counseling Center, free of charge.
- Apply for financial aid and scholarships.
- Visit Career Services.
- Use a planner to record assignments and test dates.

SURVIVE

the

TRANSITION

REMEMBER HOW YOU FELT ON THE FIRST DAY OF

classes at your current college? Wrenching adjustments? Confused? Disoriented? Uncertain? Shy? Low profile? Didn't want to look like a newcomer. Didn't want to look like you didn't fit. Didn't want to look stupid. Didn't want to look naïve. Whether or not you enjoyed high school, at least there were familiar faces of students, teachers, coaches, even the principal and cafeteria staff. Not here, not now. Even if a lot of your friends were freshmen at the same college, strangers far outnumbered them. Maybe you were lucky enough to attend one of the handful of colleges that offer optional semester-long courses to help freshmen adapt in their first year.

COPING WITH CHANGE

Fast forward to your first day as a transfer student: The new setting is a psychological one, not merely a geographic or physical one. A sense of isolation isn't unusual. On one hand, you're now more self-confident, more adaptable, and more self-directed than you were at seventeen or eighteen. On the other hand, this *is* a time of transition. Even if you'd visited the new campus a couple of times during the scoping-out and application process and even if you attended orientation, unfamiliar faces outnumber familiar ones. And unlike freshman year, most fellow students in your classes will be old hands who already know their way around and can blend in. As a result, there are different challenges to face, different worries to cope with, and different pressures to handle.

"If you prefer a small, cozy school, it will take time at a bigger university," says a student who switched from Lansing Community College (Michigan) to Michigan State University. "If you're coming from a small two-year college, it's a big adjustment. Everything is bigger, and as a student you can feel less significant within a 'big' university."

Past successes don't shield you from the realities of change. For instance, when a defensive tackle who transferred from a two-year college in Arizona arrived at the University of Florida, he quickly discovered that "everything's faster. It's a lot more competitive. Everybody's stronger and quicker."

A student transferring from Collin County Community College (Texas) worried about her ability to handle new and heavier academic demands after what she considered a less-than-challenging three years: "My major concern is adapting to a harder class load. I am concerned that I may not be prepared for the workload of a four-year college."

Such concerns are natural. It's not unusual for prospective transfer students to admit—at least to themselves and to close friends—how uncertain they are about getting used to their new environment. Orientation and a careful review of Web and printed materials can prepare you in part for these megachanges but won't eliminate the personal obligation to take control of your life. And beyond orientation and the availability of counselors, your new college probably won't offer a formal, ongoing program to ease the transition.

Colleges want you to flourish and succeed, and many gamble that you will, even if your record so far has been shaky. A California legislative analysis reported that a majority of transfer students lack college-level math and writing skills when they arrive at California State University and University of California campuses, but that doesn't mean they won't graduate. Such research findings do encourage colleges to develop remedial and support programs to help transfers overcome such shortcomings and make a successful transition to a more competitive and demanding environment.

FINDING A FACULTY MENTOR

One approach that eases transition is finding a faculty mentor, either formal or informal, to discuss academic and personal concerns with. Success in college correlates closely with solid student-faculty connections, in the classroom and beyond.

Richard Light, a Harvard University (Massachusetts) education professor who oversaw a ten-year study of more than sixteen hundred Harvard students, says the research confirmed the importance of a strong faculty relationship. The research produced a book, *Making the Most of College* (Harvard University Press, latest edition). Light tells each of his advisees at the start of each semester, "Your job is to get to know one faculty member reasonably well and get that faculty member to know you reasonably well. If you do nothing else, do that."

An effective mentor need not be designated as your official advisor, but that doesn't mean his or her advice and perspectives will be any less valuable. First look in your own department. There may be an instructor whose research interests match your own, or somebody who impressed you during an orientation presentation, or somebody you heard praised by another student, or somebody you read about in the campus paper. It could also be somebody who's teaching a course you're now taking.

If you don't find anybody you're comfortable with inside your department, check other programs or departments related to your interests. Say you're a history major interested in international relations. You may find a kindred faculty soul in political science, foreign languages, history, regional studies, or sociology. In fact, you may feel freer to speak candidly to somebody outside your own department.

You're not limited to on-campus mentoring. For example, you can find a member of the clergy or spiritual advisor on or off campus. Again, you're looking for somebody to build an ongoing relationship with, someone you can respect, and somebody you'll feel comfortable with in discussing personal concerns, doubts, and experiences.

OTHER TYPES OF SUPPORT

Diana Guerrero, the director of admissions at the University of Texas at El Paso, says, "Students also benefit from support groups such as transfer student associations." One such program, the student-run Ithaca College (New York) Transfer Community, uses former transfer students to mentor new ones. The group also participates in community service and activism.

"Become physically comfortable in the new surroundings."

—Patricia Brewer, assistant to the vice president for instruction,
Sinclair Community College (Ohio)

Transfer shock: **When students move from one kind of educational experience to another, they sometimes find the transition to be more difficult than they thought it would be. While many transfer students adapt quickly and enjoy the new environment, others may feel lonely and unsure. Researchers have studied this experience and have labeled it "transfer shock." A common result is a drop in grades in the first year after transfer. In rare cases, the transition can be so distressing that those students get discouraged and drop out.**

But it doesn't have to be like that. The good news is—once these students adjust, their grades go back up. So if you experience some transfer shock, try the things other students have found helpful. And hang in there. It will get better.

—British Columbia Council on Admissions and Transfer

Athletes face an additional set of transfer challenges as they adjust not only to new faculty, new courses, new classmates, and a new campus, but also to new teams, new teammates, new coaches, and new playing styles. Transfers from one National College Athletic Association Division I school to another also generally face a year on the bench.

Expect adjustment time. Bruce Weber, the head basketball coach at Southern Illinois University, told the campus newspaper, "Usually it takes a junior-college kid somewhere between half a season and a season, and then they adjust to the level."

The *Daily Northwestern,* the campus paper at Northwestern University (Illinois), interviewed four basketball players who transferred at the same time, but to different schools. The one who moved to Wake Forest University (North Carolina) described how he "felt like a freshman again." The one who went to Drake University (Iowa) admitted that he had second-guessed his decision for the first few months but now believes a transfer was necessary and "has a new family now." The third ended up at Creighton University (Nebraska), a school with a smaller, closer-knit atmosphere near his hometown. The fourth switched to South

Dakota State University, an NCAA Division II college, where he was eligible to compete immediately. "It's more on my level and it gave me the opportunity to step in and help my team right away, instead of having to sit back and watch and wait for my turn."

DISCOVER THE COMMUNITY

Explore. A successful transition enables you to learn about the community and what it offers. Get a map. Walk around or ride the buses. Check out the malls, the boutiques, the bookstores, the cafés, the movie theaters, the parks, the zoos, and the beaches. If there are professional major league or minor league sports in the area, take in a game. If you golf, check out the courses. If you ski, check out the slopes. If you skate, check out the rinks. Take in a concert, an art gallery, or a play. Find out about local festivals, fairs, and celebrations.

Remember the restaurants. If you get tired of dorm food, fast food, chains, or your own cooking, it's handy to know about alternatives such as ethnic restaurants, or upscale spots for special occasions.

Don't ignore the public libraries, which are valuable assets in many communities and may have material that's not available on campus. College students often use local public libraries for studying and research.

GET INVOLVED

How *will* you fit in? How *will* you meet a variety of people? How *will* you enrich your experiences and your education beyond the classroom and the library? How *will* you fill your spare time without wasting it on junk TV shows and marathon video game sessions?

One of the best ways to answer those questions is to join at least one organization. If you're not by personality a joiner, start gingerly by attending a couple of meetings or activities before deciding whether you feel comfortable with the members and whether the group's focus interests you. Consider options from different arenas. One may revolve around your spiritual or ethnic identity. Another may tie into your political and public affairs interests. One may focus on physical recreation or outdoor recreation or student government. Still another may be purely social. The British Columbia Council on Admissions and Transfer reports that "researchers have found that students who make an effort to reach out to others enjoy their time more and do better in their studies."

Some colleges put a heightened emphasis on extracurricular involvement. The State University of New York at Plattsburgh produces an official "co-curricular transcript" listing each student's out-of-class activities and the corresponding skills each has developed as a result. "The document encourages greater awareness of how a student is investing her or his time, strengths and limits, accomplishments, and progress toward life and career goals," according to the college. "This awareness can help students to more intentionally choose activities that enhance their development."

Remember, there are lots of roles to play within an organization. Not all members of a campus theater group want to appear on stage. Others design and build sets, make costumes, help with makeup, run the lighting and sound systems, sell tickets, play in the pit orchestra, raise money, work on publicity, and serve as ushers.

Each person has a personal studying style. Some do best on their own, while others learn more easily when they study in collaboration with others. If you fall into the second category, take part in study groups for your courses, and don't wait until the day before the midterm or until the point in the semester at which your grade is already in the toilet. You'll find yourself amid other motivated students who recognize the importance of cooperation and collaboration in the learning process. If there isn't a study group yet for a course, volunteer to organize one. If existing study groups are too large to be useful, help set up a new one. Even if you didn't participate in study groups at your previous college, they can simultaneously help you fit in on the new campus and do the best possible job academically.

Play intramural sports. Head to the gym, courts, or fitness center for pick-up games of basketball, volleyball, or racquet sports. See if there are leagues. As you work out with weights or jog around the track, talk to other students doing the same thing.

Try a free or low-cost, noncredit lifestyle course like yoga, aerobics, line dancing, introductory guitar, gourmet cooking, or crafts. They're a welcome relief from day-to-day academic pressures, and everybody is there by choice.

Attend plays, films, lectures, and concerts on campus. They'll be free or inexpensive. You'll not only enrich your mind and relax, but also have a chance to meet people with similar interests.

Volunteer to tutor or to work on campus environmental and improvement projects. Beyond the contacts you make and the résumé-boosting potential of volunteer service, there's a deep emotional satisfaction in giving of yourself.

Consider opportunities for involvement in campus media. Even if writing does not interest you, the college paper, yearbook, or literary magazine may benefit from your graphic design or photography skills. If the journalism or programming aspects of the newspaper and broadcast station don't interest you, your business and marketing skills can sell ads.

Take advantage of housing-related opportunities where you'll automatically have a shared interest in the quality of life. Many counselors strongly suggest that transfer students live on campus at the start if that option is available. Gustavus Adolphus College (Minnesota) recommends, "As a transfer student, you are encouraged to live on campus." And Bradley University (Illinois) says, "Transfer students gain particular advantage by choosing a university residence hall."

If you do live on campus, dormitories and student apartment complexes have committees dealing with social activities, sports, and residence hall governance. They may sponsor dances, yoga and fitness workouts, parties, and intramural teams, among other programs, to help residents get acquainted in a casual setting.

"My suggestion for transfers is to get involved in activities that interest you right away. It helps you to make friends quickly and find people with common interests. And it helps the transition into a new place."

—Transfer student at Wake Forest University (North Carolina)

Take advantage of the resident advisors in your dorm. Although they're students too, they're trained to help you cope with adjustment problems such as homesickness, roommate conflicts, or peer pressure.

If you live in a fraternity or sorority house or in a cooperative, you'll find yourself in the midst of a network of people to relax with, to confide in, and to do things with.

Even if you live independently in an off-campus apartment or house, there may be a neighborhood or block association involved with such issues as housing conditions, local parks, neighborhood safety, traffic, or parking. They may hold block parties or other social gatherings, as well as sponsor anticrime neighborhood watch programs.

Worried that extracurricular activities will distract you from studying and hurt your grades? Such concerns may not be warranted, especially if you exercise self-control and manage your time effectively.

Professor Richard Light, who studied students at Harvard University (Massachusetts) for a decade, says students who get involved are happier than those who don't, even if their chosen activities don't bolster a résumé or improve the odds of a graduate school acceptance. According to a *New York Times* account of his reseach project and findings, "Students who have worked hard to get into college, Professor Light said, tend to arrive and say, 'Academic work is my priority, and doing other things will hurt that.' In fact, the Harvard research found otherwise. 'What goes on in situations outside of class is just as important, and in some situations, it turns out to be a bigger deal than what happens in class. Very often an experience outside of class can have a profound effect on the courses students choose and even what they want to do with their lives.'"

USE THE SUMMER

If you expect to start at your new college for the fall semester, consider making the move in time to take summer courses there.

That could give you an advantage in the transition process. First, summers tend to be more relaxed and less crowded on campus, reducing the stress—especially if you're heading from a small school to a large one. Although fewer courses are offered, classes frequently are smaller than during the fall and spring. Second, you'll get a head start in understanding the new school's approach to academics. Third, you may be able to fulfill prerequisites or take required courses, getting them out of the way before the fall. Fourth, you can hunt early for a part-time job and for housing. And fifth, you'll have more time to become familiar with the campus and community.

At some colleges, including Rochester Institute of Technology (New York), there are degree programs that offer summer transfer adjustment. Participation may be compulsory for admission to certain programs.

INVOLVEMENT OFF CAMPUS

Don't ignore the "outside"—meaning noncollege—world. Getting involved can pay off in several ways. From an immediate perspective, it's a great way to meet people, to feel like you belong, and to widen your vistas beyond classes and students. There's the psychic satisfaction of contributing brains and energy to something that matters to you and to other people. There's the prospect of networking that can lead to paid part-time or full-time employment. There's the bolstering of your résumé. And there's the building of skills that can help you in your academic and career plans. In addition, many students find that their community volunteer experiences provide rich grist for the mill of term papers, class projects, and other academic assignments.

Since only a minority of colleges have mandatory community service requirements, in most instances it's up to you to take the initiative and reach out. Here are some of the best ways to find such opportunities:

FOCUS ON ACTIVITIES THAT MOST INTEREST YOU

Often these will be logical extensions of things you've done in the past. If you were a Boy Scout, a Girl Scout, or a 4-H or FFA member, the local community can provide a forum to continue your involvement, this time as an adult leader. If you've previously performed or worked with music, dance, or theater, you can find local concert and jazz bands, theater troupes, dance companies, choral groups, and orchestras. If you volunteered before at a hospital, nursing home, day-care center, or senior citizen center, your experience and enthusiasm will be welcome at similar institutions near campus. If you helped out in political campaigns back home or at your former college, major party, third party, and independent candidates and officeholders will welcome your involvement. If you played sports, look for chances to coach elementary and middle school kids on community-based teams. If you enjoy bicycling, bowling, sailing, running marathons, or other recreational activities, find community-based groups of like-minded individuals that sponsor outings, leagues, and competitions.

For many transfer students, the first off-campus involvement is tied to their religious or faith-based beliefs. They look for a church, mosque, synagogue, or other religious institution that feels welcoming—a spiritual home—to them. They get to know local families, perhaps volunteer to help teach religious lessons, join religious studies classes, and serve as youth group advisors.

For many others, that initial involvement can arise from their racial, national, or ethnic identity, and they find companionship by becoming associated with related community centers and organizations.

THINK ABOUT SKILLS AND INTERESTS YOU'D LIKE TO DEVELOP

Say you're considering a teaching career. Instead of waiting until your formal classroom observation courses and student teaching, contact nearby public and private schools to volunteer as a tutor or reading coach. If you're looking at psychology, social work, or counseling, consider suicide hotlines, shelters for battered women or the homeless, or substance abuse programs. That way you have a chance to be of service while getting a better sense of whether those career plans in the abstract match reality. Maybe you hope to go into nursing, medicine, dentistry, physical therapy, or another health area. If so, hospitals, clinics, and similar institutions can use volunteers. Thinking about veterinary medicine, zoology, or a similar field? Volunteer at the local animal shelter or humane society.

ASK ABOUT VOLUNTEERING

Ask whether the college has a volunteer clearinghouse or information center and visit it. This type of service matches would-be volunteers with charitable and area groups seeking assistance. Here you'll find listings that describe participating organizations and explain the skills they want, expected time commitments, and level of responsibility. The center staff can also answer questions that will help you find an appropriate placement.

Some college-affiliated groups have ongoing partnerships with the community. These might take the form of "adopting" a park or stretch of road for periodic cleanups, regularly providing a cadre of tutors for a nearby elementary school, or staffing events such as fund-raising bike rides, road races, and blood drives.

Then plunge in. Telephone the organization, agency, or school to make an appointment with the volunteer coordinator. Don't make a commitment until you have a clear understanding of what your duties will be and you've had a chance to talk with the staff and observe the operation.

You need to set priorities, but also remember that college is about more than studying, and there's plenty to learn that doesn't relate directly to your course work. At the same time, don't overload yourself with too many commitments that will undermine your studies and academic priorities.

COMMON MISTAKES

What are the most common mistakes and oversights that transfer students make in preparing themselves for the transition?

THINKING THAT THEIR NEW COLLEGE WILL BE JUST LIKE THE PREVIOUS ONE
As a transfer recruiter at Fresno Pacific University (California) puts it, "Students assume that the culture and expectations of the institution that they're transferring to are similar to where they're currently attending."

Some students hold the misperception that a university is the same as—or at least similar to—a community or junior college. In reality, even if you move from one community college to another, from one small private four-year college to another, or from one large state university to another, each has a different institutional personality and mix of faculty, students, and staff. Knowing about one is *not* the same as knowing about another.

On the academic front, you'll discover variations in study expectations, grading practices, class size, teaching styles, access to faculty, even intellectual challenge.

Academic expectations may differ. On the lifestyle front, you'll experience distinctions in social mores, housing patterns, diversity, acceptance of alternative relationships, and amount of part-time employment, even spirituality. On the extracurricular front, you'll find differences in the degree of student involvement, the range of organizations, time demands, even respect for the value of outside activities.

Don't assume that the rules and regulations will be the same either. Codes of conduct, minimum grade requirements to avoid academic probation or suspension, intellectual integrity, and regulations for behavior in dormitories are among the areas that change from college to college. So do complaint procedures, including the availability of a college ombuds office, a campus disciplinary system, and a procedure for appealing grades.

The solution requires developing a full understanding of your new school, maintaining an open mind—"it's not better, it's just different"—and an evolution in your own mind-set.

FAILURE TO TAKE TIME TO EDUCATE THEMSELVES
ABOUT THEIR NEW INSTITUTION

If you didn't do your homework in targeting schools, it's inevitable you'll confront unanticipated roadblocks once you arrive. They may involve classes and majors, financial matters, campus environment, student and faculty diversity, and extracurricular programs, among others. Perhaps you were wearing rose-colored glasses, relied on gossip from friends, unquestioningly believed the fond reminiscences of gray-haired alumni, fell for an overblown reputation, or were seduced by your own ego.

The solution includes a preorientation visit to the campus if you've never been there, a careful reading of the catalog, course, and departmental descriptions, and evaluation of your chosen major and college graduation requirements. If you feel the fit won't be right, don't feel obligated to attend. Instead, take another semester to look for a more suitable institution.

POOR ACADEMIC PREPARATION

Even if you consistently received good grades in the past, your new college may place heavier academic demands on its students. In addition, the workload for advanced-level courses tends to be more rigorous than in introductory courses. You may have felt classes in the first year or two were a breeze and that you could do well with little studying, and as a result failed to develop efficient and effective study habits.

The solution includes seeking assistance from faculty members and academic advisors as soon as problems develop, forming or joining study groups, and using on-campus resources such as tutoring services, the writing center, counseling offices, and reference librarians.

WORKING TOO MANY HOURS

Most students who work do so for financial reasons—to pay their way through school or cover at least part of their expenses. If you worked long hours at your job—or jobs—at your current school but still earned satisfactory grades, you may expect to do the same after you transfer. That might prove true—but you could be in for the proverbial rude awakening in the form of exhaustion, stress, and disappointingly low marks.

The solution includes a realistic assessment or reassessment of your job commitments soon after you transfer. You might need to cut back on hours but work more during vacations and the summer to cover the financial loss. Depending on your financial situation and obligations, you may choose to borrow more money, reduce the number of credit hours per semester, or search for a higher-paying part-time job.

A successful transition won't happen magically. You must make the psychic effort for it to work.

"Take it one day at a time. There are some days when you'll just need to put the book down and go out. It's the days when you don't need to but do it anyway that you'll have to make up for."

—Transfer student at Michigan State University

CONCLUSION

HERE ARE FIVE FINAL REMINDERS:

- *Be smart for the sake of your future:* Do research. Ask questions. Work hard. Keep your eyes and ears open. Don't make rash decisions. Plan. Trust yourself and your goals. Figure out what you want. Assess your skills and aspirations.

- *Understand the process:* Figure out and follow the proper application procedures. Don't overlook any steps. Take the clues and suggestions when something isn't required. Meet all deadlines.

- *Be realistic—and ambitious:* Remember that horizons are wide, possibilities virtually limitless. Don't sell yourself short. Consider alternatives. Focus on ways to overcome perceived obstacles. Hedge your bets.

- *Be desirable:* Remember that colleges *want* transfer students. Build achievements, then highlight them. Market your abilities. Make it as tough as possible for them to reject you.

- *Make it work:* Once you've been accepted to a new college, do all in your power to succeed there. Be flexible. Be motivated. Be open. Be patient.

Although transferring is a labor-intensive process, it's also a means of discovery. Through it, you'll learn not only about colleges and courses and opportunities in and out of class, but also about yourself—your capabilities your dreams, your potential for growth, your openness to ideas. The payoff will last a lifetime.

GLOSSARY

Accreditation: Certification by a professional association that a college, department, or program meets or exceeds minimum standards for quality.

Articulation agreements: Contracts or arrangements among colleges to recognize each other's courses for purposes such as transfer credits and prerequisites. These are also known as credit transfer agreements.

Certificate of Financial Responsibility: Certification and documentation that an international student has enough money to cover educational and living expenses while studying in the United States.

College Level Examination Program (CLEP): A national testing program that determines whether students are eligible for college credit based on their past learning, noncredit courses, advanced high school classes, and independent study. Each college decides whether to accept CLEP results.

Credit for Prior Learning: A program that grants credit based on what a student has previously learned. It may use varying formats including College Level Examination Program testing, departmental exams, portfolio assessments, individualized appraisals, and military course evaluations.

Credit evaluation: A college's review of a student's past academic course work at another school to determine which credits and courses to recognize.

Credit transfer agreements: *See* Articulation agreements.

Expected Family Contribution: The amount of money a student's family is expected to provide each year toward his or her higher education. It's based on a federal government formula set by Congress and it considers such factors as income, savings, investments, and the number of family members in college at the time.

Free Application for Federal Student Aid (FAFSA): The U.S. Department of Education form that most colleges use to determine eligibility for financial aid such as scholarships, loans, grants, and work-study jobs.

I-20: The U.S. Immigration and Naturalization Service's certification of an international student's eligibility for a nonimmigrant visa.

Legacies: Students whose parents, grandparents, or other relatives are alumni of the same college.

Portfolio: A sampling that showcases a student's creative work, such as drawings, poems, photographs, musical compositions, short stories, or paintings.

Quality points: A formula that considers both the grade and the number of credits in previous courses to help evaluate a transfer applicant's past academic performance. The calculation generally involves multiplying the number of credits times the grade. For example, a four-credit course with a 3.0 would be worth twelve quality points, but the same course with a 2.0 would earn only eight quality points.

Rolling admissions: The process of making acceptance or rejection decisions as applications arrive without waiting for the application deadline. With rolling admissions, all transfer slots might be filled before every application is processed and evaluated.

INDEX

M

Macalester College (MN), 45
majors
  application requirements for, 125–27
  checking out departments, 83–86
Marlboro College (VT), 68, 227
Massachusetts Institute of Technology, 146
McGill University (QC), 123
Memorial University of Newfoundland,
  191–92
Mercy College (NY), 44
Miami University (FL), 144
Michigan State University, 46, 154–55,
  191, 202
military veterans
  military educational credits, 171
  ROTC scholarships for, 203
  support services for, 71
minority students, placement and career-
  planning services for, 69
mission statements, 44–45
Mississippi State University, 209
Missouri, A+ program, 25
Money magazine, 51
Montana State University, 169
Morehouse College (GA), 20, 147
Mount Holyoke College (MA), 22, 59

N

National Association of Intercollegiate
  Athletics (NAIA), 26–27, 65
National Collegiate Athletics Association
  (NCAA), 26–27, 65
New England Board of Higher Education,
  Regional Student Program, 209
1974 Family Educational Rights and
  Privacy Act, 153
nontraditional grading systems, 69
nontraditional students
  admission decisions, 11
  characteristics of, 21
  transitional programs for, 13–15

North Dakota State University, 209
Northeastern University (MA), 91
nursing students, ROTC scholarships
  for, 203

O

Oberlin College (OH), 161–62
off-campus community
  exploring, 107, 232
  involvement in, 245–47
off-campus housing
  aspects of, 219
  checking out, 68
Oglala Lakota College (SD), 46
Ohio State University at Columbus, 173
on-campus housing
  application for, 218–22
  checking out, 67, 108
online courses, 93–94
orientation program
  academic considerations, 226–27
  attending social events at, 232
  benefits of attending, 225–26
  checking out facilities and services,
    230–31
  employment opportunities, 228–29
  exploring off-campus community, 232
  extracurricular opportunities, 227
  finalizing housing arrangements, 230
  financial aid and, 229–30
  for international students, 231
  rules and regulations, 228
overseas study, 88

P

parenting services, 70
Parent Loans for Undergraduate
  Students (PLUS), 189
period studies programs, 87
placement and career-planning centers,
  69–70, 109

OTHER BOOKS ON COLLEGE AND BEYOND

Cool Colleges: *For the Hyper-Intelligent, Self-Directed, Late Blooming, and Just Plain Different*
by Don Asher
Finding an unconventional college that reflects your unique sense of style and adventure—that's impossible. Or is it? This unprecedented guide profiles the most innovative and unusual schools in the country.
8 x 10 inches, 464 pages
$19.95 (Can $30.95)
ISBN 1-58008-150-9

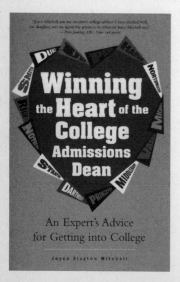

Winning the Heart of the College Admissions Dean: *An Expert's Advice for Getting into College*
by Joyce Slayton Mitchell
This insightful guide, based on thirty-five years of college counseling success, will walk you through the process of finding the right college, standing out from the crowd, and winning the heart of the college admissions dean.
6 x 9 inches, 208 pages
$14.95 (Can $20.95)
ISBN 1-58008-300-5

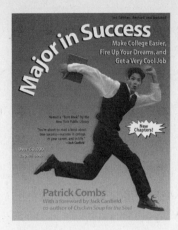

Major in Success: *Make College Easier, Fire Up Your Dreams, and Get a Very Cool Job*
by Patrick Combs

With great job and internship ideas, smart strategies for overcoming fears, hot tips on interviewing, and the best job-hunting Web sites, this savvy and inspiring guide will help you discover your passions and excel in life.

7³⁄₈ x 9¹⁄₄ inches, 192 pages

$12.95 (Can $20.95)

ISBN 1-58008-209-2

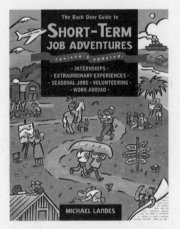

The Backdoor Guide to Short-Term Job Adventures
by Michael Landes

This incredible resource lists over 1,000 work-and-learn adventures, including internships, seasonal work, volunteer opportunities, and overseas jobs.

8³⁄₈ x 10⁷⁄₈ inches, 336 pages

$19.95 (Can $30.95)

ISBN 1-58008-147-9

Available from your local bookstore, or by ordering direct from the publisher.

TEN SPEED PRESS / CELESTIAL ARTS / TRICYCLE PRESS

P.O. Box 7123, Berkeley, CA 94707

Phone (800) 841-2665 / Fax (510) 559-1629

order@tenspeed.com / www.tenspeed.com

ABOUT THE AUTHOR

Pulitzer Prize–winner Eric Freedman, J.D., teaches journalism at Michigan State University. He is a graduate of Cornell University and New York University Law School, and has done additional graduate work at Michigan State. He is the author or coauthor of five previous books including *What to Study: 101 Fields in a Flash,* and serves as a senior writer for *Community College Week.* His articles have appeared in more than 125 publications around the world including *Careers & Colleges* and *Black Issues in Higher Education.*